D0115784

LEVERAGE

How to Create Your Own "Tipping Points" in Business and in Life

LEVERAGE

How to Create Your Own
"Tipping Points"
in Business and in Life

By Darby Checketts
Foreword by Steve Chandler

CAREER
PRESS
Franklin Lakes, N.J.

LEVERAGE

EDITED AND TYPESET BY GINA TALUCCI

Cover design by Jeffrey Bailey/Solaris Design Group

Printed in the U.S.A. by Book-mart Press

To order this title, please call toll-free 1-800-CAREER-1 (NJ and Canada: 201-848-0310) to order using VISA or MasterCard, or for further information on books from Career Press.

The Career Press, Inc., 3 Tice Road, PO Box 687,
Franklin Lakes, NJ 07417
www.careerpress.com

Library of Congress Cataloging-in-Publication Data

Checketts, Darby

Leverage : how to create your own "tipping points" in business and in life / by Darby Checketts.

p. cm.

Includes index.

ISBN-13: 978-1-56414-870-4 (hardcover)

ISBN-10: 1-56414-870-X (hardcover)

1. Leadership. I. Title.

HD57.7.C482 2006
658.4' 092--dc22

2005058101

Dedication

The greatest test of our faith is when we fall down and rise up, again. During the writing of this book, there have been many calamities in the world...in Iraq, Southeast Asia, India, Great Britain, Niger, Sudan, Pakistan, the United States of America, and more. This book is dedicated to *survivors*—those who rise up and rebuild—and to those who tirelessly help them. Together with these heroes, we can all lift the world a little higher than before. Our courage and faith will sustain us. Our ingenuity will combine with leverage of all kinds to make the impossible possible. Calamities are tipping points for humanity. These bring out the best we have to offer each other. Then, the dream goes on and we move forward once again.

Acknowledgments

A great friend of mind once reminded me, "Darby, you can have all the talent in the world, but until someone gives you the opportunity to use it, it's not of much value." I always say that many of us go to our graves with their music still inside. It should be a goal for each of us to "get the music out."

I offer profound thanks to my publisher, Career Press, for helping me put my talent to use and get my "music" out to do the good it is intended to do. Michael Pye has been my co-visionary. Ron Fry leads the team. Gina Talucci became my partner as we entered the vital realm of layout and final edits. And I thank Kristen Parkes, Jeff Piasky, and others who made the book a quality product that we can all enjoy.

Thanks to my fantastic coach and colleague, Steve Chandler, who tells me that I'm no longer Lancelot and

I must now choose to be King Arthur or Merlin. Steve says Merlin may be most appropriate. What an honor it is to be considered experienced enough to have some wisdom that is of value to the world. I thank those who have contributed to that wisdom by allowing me to be in your lives, by lifting me, and by letting me lift you in some way. It is a cascade of wisdom that has blessed us all. Sharon Checketts is my most trustworthy companion and the single greatest blessing in my life. Our children, Natalie, Vance, Denise, Cheryl, Ken, Brent, and Matt have become *my* heroes. My dear mother, Patricia; my generous father, Widtsoe; and my seven siblings created the loving launch pad that I needed.

Over the years, my clients have been a major factor in my professional growth, experience, and wisdom. Thanks for the trust and for the opportunities to serve.

Three other individuals have also been my mentors in the business of leading, teaching, coaching, and helping to lift others. Ed Yager, thanks for pointing the way. John Arnold, thanks for the sheer energy. Gene Mondani, thanks for believing in me all these years.

Thanks to my dear friends in Nigeria: Caleb Yaro, Peter Madike, and Charles Cudjoe. In all my travels, the West African chapter of my life has never been equaled in terms of cross-cultural learning and the many expressions of generosity and trust. I also express appreciation for the genuine hospitality shown to me by my Muslim associates in Nigeria. As we would meet together, our religious differences were "points of interest" and not a cause for conflict. We found the common ground upon which we could build friendship.

Others have been friends to me in ways that make me eternally grateful: Myrna Lea Houston, Lawrence Towver, Andy Allen, Ray Kettering, George Anderson, Lynn Fairbanks, Gary Allen, Dave Witt, Fred Barnett, Steve Hatch, and many others who must trust my heart, if not my memory.

Thank you, Archimedes, for the metaphor. It is the source of the inspiration for 25 keys to greater leverage, and for everyone who reads this book.

Finally, thank you, dear God, for giving me time to write this book of my life and for granting Archimedes permission to help.

Contents

Foreword by Steve Chandler   15

Preface: The Archimedes Factor   19

Note to the Reader   25

Leverage Key 1:   Close to Kilimanjaro?   27

Leverage Key 2:   Life Is Better
                      With Bookends   35

Leverage Key 3:   The Five Arenas of Life 45

Leverage Key 4:   Listen for the
                      Voice of the Cricket   57

Leverage Key 5:   Who in the World
Is Out There?   63

Leverage Key 6:   Vision: Demystify It
and Go There   69

Leverage Key 7:   Principle-Centered:
Do the Right Thing!   75

Leverage Key 8:   Fuel With Desire,
Passion, and Determination   81

Leverage Key 9:   What Must I Give
to Succeed?   89

Leverage Key 10:   The Best Investment
You'll Ever Make   95

Leverage Key 11:   The Big Picture:
CombiningDirection
With Perspective   103

Leverage Key 12:   Ownership and
Stewardship   111

Leverage Key 13:   Leadership and
Influence   119

Leverage Key 14:   Truth   127

Leverage Key 15:   Force Fields   131

Leverage Key 16:   Commitment   139

Leverage Key 17:   Agreement   147

Leverage Key 18: Thinking   151

Leverage Key 19: Learning   159

Leverage Key 20: Mechanisms   167

Leverage Key 21: Partnerships   173

Leverage Key 22: Money and Wealth   181

Leverage Key 23: Exuberance   189

Leverage Key 24: What's Love Got to
                    Do With It?   195

Leverage Key 25: Your Value Proposition   201

Conclusion   207

The Genesis of a Book   211

Index   215

About the Author   221

Foreword

To most people, it might not occur to them to lift their world. To many people, the world is what lifts *them*, then sometimes drops them, and leaves them singing those same old victim songs such as, "Stop the world, I want to get off!"

Darby Checketts has written a book to change that. He has written a book that shows us where our levers are, for every situation. At the focal point of every so-called problem, *there is a lever*. And if we will only take it up in our hands, we could *lift* our world instead of being overwhelmed and frightened by it.

What is most useful and inspiring about this book *Leverage* is that it gives us specific gripping points to hold on to. *Good to Great*, by Jim Collins, was a great book, but it was centered in the labyrinthine world of corporations. It did not suggest a way to boost *yourself* from good to great. *Leverage* does.

The Tipping Point was a fascinating study of the mysterious moment inside events that change their nature completely. It is full of insight and yet it didn't tell you, personally, how to *generate* those key moments in your life. *Leverage* does. This book doesn't leave your tipping points to outside forces. It takes the mystery out.

Darby Checketts is a masterful teacher and coach. I have had the pleasure of seeing him work in person. He is a gifted public speaker whose innovative programs for Customer Astonishment have been morphed, borrowed from, saluted, used, copied, honored, and implemented by some of the brightest stars on the success horizon. In person, he is a spellbinder. Even on a conference phone call, he produces transformation. He is leverage itself.

In this book, Darby Checketts has taken the profound insight of Archimedes and brought it right smack into a futuristic context. The speedy world we live in today is all about leverage. Those who have leverage win—those who don't stay stuck down below in their immovable worlds.

So, to now be able to hold in my hands in book form the heart and soul of this good man's life, wisdom and excitement about lifting both your world and *the* world, I am blessed. You will be, too. So, feast on this book. Underline, highlight, and mark it up. Then, buy a new clean copy for your dearest friend. Let your friend's world be lifted, too.

With this book you will see how to go from good to great, and how to create your own tipping points in every area of your life. Success is not about wealth or circumstance; it's about seizing a lever long enough to lift your world and then just go on lifting. There's a single word to describe what *you* will become once you master the 25 easy keys to leverage in these pages: Uplifting.

Steve Chandler
Phoenix, Arizona

Preface

The Archimedes Factor

Down one side street and then another....Plastered walls, sandstone color; one shop looked just like the other. The weather was warm and humid. "Keep going," they said. "There's delicious, authentic Greek food. Keep going. It's straight ahead." After touring the city on foot for several hours, I was starving. All I could think of was a gyro sandwich smothered in onions and sour cream, accompanied by an ice-cold drink. I finally found the cafe. "No lamb, no gyros, just fish today," the café owner announced. "Okay, I'll have the fish." I sat all alone in the café as I soaked up the idea that I was in the ancient, great city of Athens.

Just minutes earlier, I had been standing on the steps of the Parthenon. As a trainer and professional speaker I wondered what the acoustics would have been like for a seminar long, long ago. Perhaps the guest speaker would be my new hero, Archimedes. I can picture him now with the white tunic, leather sash, sandals, jet-black hair, suntanned skin, slightly wrinkled face, medium build, and a brisk gait. The study of physics and mathematics suggested to me a man who took life seriously.

Archimedes Will Speak Today

The dream became clearer to me....Feet shuffled, dust rose from the floor, and the sun began to set. The moderator announced, "Archimedes will speak today." There were some whispers about the possible nature of his remarks. Even the most serious of Greek philosophers could be easily bored, I am sure. Mathematics makes the world go around, but there'd better be something new in today's lecture, they thought. Already known for his water displacement and weight measurement formulas, Archimedes chose to digress from his usual discourse. Today, in true Greek fashion, he would wax philosophical. He climbed the stone steps to the podium and held up a large glass sphere for all to behold. It was bold that he chose a sphere, for his colleagues still debated the shape of the earth. Many hundreds of years would pass before Archimedes' beliefs would be put to the full test. He stood and finally said:

> *See our earth. It is immense beyond belief. It is beautiful with hues of brown, blue, and green. What a wonder it must be to view from the*

thrones of the Gods. It is complex. Its geography, its rhythms, and its denizens challenge our understanding. In its movement from day into night, it obeys some grand celestial law we cannot comprehend. But...there are forces we see all around us from which we begin to learn more.

Then, he moved to a table near the podium and began a clever demonstration.

Mathematicians and physicists know well the principle of lever and fulcrum. Take this orb, place it here, and put the small wedge or fulcrum somewhat near it. Then, with this lever lift it so gently. The closer the fulcrum to the lifter, the shorter his effective lever will be and the less power he will possess. Move the fulcrum farther, then farther beyond him to extend his leverage and his power will be magnified again and again. Give me a lever long enough and a place to stand, and I could lift the world. I could lift the world.

Archimedes paused. There were whispers, more whispers, then finally cheers. The audience resounded, "Yes, he could lift the world, it is true. But where would he stand, that's the question?"

Astronauts Now Circle the Globe

Astronauts circle the globe many miles out into space. The earth is much smaller to them than to the

Greeks so very long ago. It is a magnificent brown, blue, and green orb partially shrouded by billowing clouds. These modern mathematicians, physicists, and explorers do have a platform to stand upon as they lift the world. Their heavenly perspective lifts the horizons of humankind and changes the course of the planet. Their lever is science. Their lever is courage. Their lever is an ever-broadening understanding of time and space and those celestial laws in operation.

Back on earth, a busy executive asks his coach, "Can you help me lift my people? They work hard. They serve their customers tirelessly and are sometimes expected to do the impossible." His coach responds, "Together, we can help them lift their worlds. They are skilled and have a sense of purpose. Their perspective is global, but they need a sense of focus. We will help them examine the core principles that guide them. They will have a firm place to stand. Then, what they'll need is more leverage. Today, we will teach of personal power and partnerships for, with the right partners, nothing is impossible in business. This is often the leverage they need most. Together, we will strengthen their sense of purpose so they can lift the world even higher."

Will You and Archimedes Lift the World?

What are your levers?

Knowledge...courage...partners on whom you rely? Is your footing solid? Are you ready to rock the world, to change it, and to lift it? Far greater than Archimedes' command of mathematics is the marvelous metaphor he has left us. He awaits the new legacy this book will create for him. He may be reading this as I write. He is smiling to think that 2,000 years after his death we now understand what his early Greek friends only glimpsed.

The Greeks thought he was speaking of lifting a mere geometric sphere. But inspired by the sunset and his vantage point on the Acropolis, he was intent on lifting the world.

Note to the Reader

With the Archimedes Factor in mind, it is the intent of this book and its 25 Keys to help you ponder and to answer two basic questions: Where do you stand and what are your levers?

- ✓ As you crystallize answers to these questions and proceed to lift your world, you will:
- ✓ Stand firmly on *Purpose*, surrounded by powerful *Principles* to guide you.
- ✓ Grasp the tools, skills, strategies, and the resources needed to leverage your personal power and create your future.
- ✓ Put your levers in motion to lift your world and bring about those amazing "tipping points" that shape the course of events, just as you envisioned.

Read and use individual *keys* one by one as you wish and as specific needs arise. There is a general pattern and rhythm to the book as a whole. Keys 1–11 create a broad perspective on *Leverage* and help you determine *where you stand.* Keys 12 to 25 will come together to represent your own personal collection of *levers for life and leadership.* The book is about preparation. It is about the important challenges and the grand opportunities on your horizon.

Darby Checketts

Leverage Key 1

Close to Kilimanjaro?

Begin with the outcome in mind. Among my life's most wonderfully gratifying and potentially perilous adventures have been several trips to Nigeria. Many people have asked how this connection came about. During the early 1990s, I regularly conducted seminars for the public and for various client groups in the United Kingdom. I truly loved the time I spent traveling from one end of the UK to the other. During a three-seminar series in London, I was particularly impressed with one participant in the very front row; a gentleman from Nigeria named Caleb Yaro. He was a senior executive with a merchant bank based in Lagos, Nigeria. Mr. Yaro took copious notes throughout each seminar day.

He attended all three days of training. To help you under-stand the ultimate significance of my acquaintance with Mr. Yaro, I need to share some important background information.

The Power of Your 150 List

When I founded our company in 1985, I looked far and wide to identify and consolidate a set of success principles that would have a lasting impact for my clients. I studied a lot information on goal achievement and time management. One of my earliest training programs was "Balancing Your Priorities for a Lifetime of Achievement." In this program, I taught the concept of a "150 List." I learned about 150 Lists from a great gentleman by the name of Rodney Brady, whom I was privileged to interview. Mr. Brady had come to my attention because of his remarkable business accomplishments and distinguished government service at an especially early age. One magazine editor asked him the secret of this success: "Mr. Brady, to what do you attribute your remarkable success so early in life? Is it a result of a high IQ? Is it about having wealthy parents or an Ivy League education?" This is my recollection of Mr. Brady's explanation…

As I was finishing high school, I decided to make early contact with one of the coaches at the college I would attend in the fall. I asked my coach what I could do to prepare myself. He gave me this instruction: 'You are a bright young man with much potential. I want you to make a list of 150 things you intend to do with your life. You are now 17 years old. If you live to be 92 years old, you'll only have to do one, two, or three items per year to complete the process. Please make your list and don't call me again until you're done.' I was very surprised by my coach's assignment. Nevertheless, I went to work on my 150 List. I struggled with it. At the end of two weeks, I had about 18 to 20 items and was very perplexed. I had written down to finish college, get a job, get married, travel to Europe, buy a car, take another trip somewhere, buy a house, get some more education, start a family, and so on. I was stumped, so I called the coach's office. The secretary answered the phone. I told her my name and asked to speak to the coach. She turned and spoke to him. I heard the coach say, 'Ask him if he's finished his 150 List. Remind him that I don't want to speak with him again until he's done.'

I was frustrated by the coach's seeming stubbornness. Being a little ticked off, I went back to work on the list with a vengeance. I began to ask neighbors and relatives where they'd been on vacations, what they did professionally and why. I began to browse the National Geographic *magazine and* The Wall Street Journal *my parents left on the coffee table in the living room. I became curious about musical instruments, hobbies, machinery, geography, languages, various scientific endeavors, and even historical events that would reveal potential adventures to add to my 150 List. Two months went by and I had created my list. The secret to my success is that I am now in my early 50s and I have accomplished well over half the list. I take two or three items from the list each year and make these my major personal goals for that year. I'm getting better and better at goal achievement. With 30-plus years to go, I plan to finish the list. This is the secret to my success, My 150 List.*

Secrets to Goal Achievement

Over the years, several principles of goal achievement have become especially obvious:

1. Only goal setters who are goal writers are truly goal achievers.
2. First you set the goal and then you see.
3. If you don't see BIG, you won't see enough.

The items on a 150 List are fundamentally *dreams*. When these are pulled into focus for the current year in which the owner of the list hopes to work on and achieve these dreams, they become *active goals*. The 150 List is a dreaming, goal-setting, and make-it-happen tool. Otherwise, if your dreams and goals are not written down, they may go the way of mere fantasies and soon be forgotten. If you are young, create your 150 List now. If you are older, you may be content with an 80 List or a 65 List, but create a list of dreams that will draw you like a magnet into your own exciting future.

The Call to Africa

So, what is the connection between the 150 List idea and my friend, Caleb Yaro? One of the most colorful and inspirational items on my 150 List is to "Climb Mount Kilimanjaro" in East Africa. What a unique and awe-inspiring mountain it is. Its setting on the eastern plains of Africa is spectacular. Its location and history are the stuff of many legends. It represents more climbable surface from the ground up than Mount Everest, though Everest is higher, of course. Those who climb Kilimanjaro are exposed to all four of the earth's climatic zones. So, as I developed my original 150 List to include visiting all seven of the earth's continents, I had to "do Kilimanjaro" as the symbolic climax of some future visit to Africa. This mountain later became Caleb's hook as he lured me to his fascinating corner of world.

At the end of the third day of training in London, Caleb approached me and said, "Mr. Checketts, thank you for the wonderful seminars. I enjoyed them very much." I was honored by his remarks and thanked him for his friendly manner and conscientious participation. He went on to say, "My people in Nigeria need your teachings. Would you be willing to come to Lagos, Nigeria, to train our management staff and our employees?" The first thoughts that raced through my mind were those of mosquitoes and of the dictatorship that had come to rule Nigeria as the result of a military coup in the not-too-distant past. I was not sure how my teachings would be received in Africa. I hesitated to respond to Caleb and yet I was intrigued. Suddenly, the vision of a great mountain popped into my mind—Kilimanjaro, Kilimanjaro, Kilimanjaro. As if awakened from a trance, I abruptly asked my new African friend, "Just how far from Mt. Kilimanjaro is Lagos, Caleb?" He grinned with a ready reply, "Darby,

Lagos is much closer to Kilimanjaro than where you now live in the United States." He had me. Africa was on my 150 List. It was inevitable. The choice had already been made. I had to go. This was my avenue to reach Mount Kilimanjaro. The journey would take me to Nigeria. I would cherish the journey for the rest of my life.

Create your 150 List. Here are some examples of the dreams found on my own 150 List and those of my children and friends:

✓ Experience the ocean more often.

✓ Take up the sport of fencing.

✓ Overcome the fear of "foreign stocks." Pick one. Invest.

✓ Help someone learn to read.

✓ Take lessons from a master chef in an Italian village.

✓ Build a backyard gazebo with an enclosure for a hot tub.

✓ Visit my congressman or congresswoman's local office.

✓ Clean out the kids' old closets. Donate the children's books to the community library or a children's charity in West Africa.

✓ Spend time somewhere under a tree composing simple poetry about what I believe to be important.

✓ Read a book on the history of the Civil War.

✓ Help my work team set a company record for on-time deliveries.

✓ Save money. Make it a lifelong habit. Start with $500.

✓ Teach a course at a community college.

✓ Explore the Rio Coco river in Nicaragua.

✓ Climb Mount Kilimanjaro.

✓ Learn to fly an airplane.

✓ Dip my hand in the Red Sea.

✓ Visit the Sacred Well of Chi-chen-itza, Mexico.

✓ Make a parachute jump.

✓ Relearn to play the clarinet.

✓ Make regular donations to the United Nations World Food Program

✓ Follow the John Muir trail.

✓ Learn Chinese.

✓ Perform 200 sits-ups and 20 pull-ups.

✓ Read the 100 Greatest Books.

First You Set the Goal and Then You See

I have yet to climb Kilimanjaro, but I have been much closer to the mountain than most. I am not finished with my list—about 80 out of 120 so far—with many powerful goal-achieving years ahead for me. It is important that my Kilimanjaro goal helped inspire my eldest son, Vance, to go. At my request, he carried a small stone from the base of the mountain to its summit and placed it there for me.

Your 150 List is an inspiration, not an obligation. It will open your eyes to adventures you would otherwise have never imagined. As a result of my Kilimanjaro vision, I have traveled throughout Nigeria, met amazing people, enjoyed unforgettable adventures, broadened my understanding of world cultures and religions, created friendships that will last forever, and had the privilege of sharing many uplifting ideas and powerful success principles with great people who are so eager to learn. They treated me as a king. One of my dearest friends to this day is Dr. Charles Cudjoe of Kaduna, Nigeria. Our professional collaboration has contributed to his successful consultancy in Nigeria and around the globe. I am grateful to Rodney Brady and to his coach for an idea that helped me transcend my fears of mosquitoes and military dictatorships to create some of the most powerful memories of my life.

Remember, first you set the goal and then you see. Archimedes would add, "To lift the world, you must see the world." I have seen the world—25 countries on five continents—thanks to my 150 List, and I am certainly inspired to lift it. I am on a continuous quest for the greater leverage with which to do it. Join me.

Leverage Key 2

Life Is Better With Bookends

Occasionally, I decide to put a few extra books on the very top of a piece of furniture. Of course, the books eventually fall over and often end up hitting me on the head to remind me of the folly of *living life without bookends*.

Your Corporate DNA

For years, I have helped my clients cultivate and align their "corporate cultures." Corporate Culture is the DNA of a company or other organization. I had one astute CEO come to me and say this, "Darby, our company has been growing rapidly. We now have about 300 employees. I realize that very soon we will have a problem trying to pass along our values to the increasing numbers of new people who are joining us. We need a clear and discernable corporate culture."

So, I define Corporate Culture as this: *The established set of principles upon which an organization of people operates. These principles are manifest in a certain pattern of behaviors. These behaviors characterize what it is the organization stands for and how those who interact with it can expect to be treated.*

Organizational Bookends

As an organization builds or stumbles upon its culture, there is eventually an opportunity to assure some level of "cultural alignment," which is to have the individuals and departments within the organization reflect certain shared values and perform with some level of consistency. I use this analogy with my clients: You wrote the book(s) on your business. You have your corporate strategy, your marketing manual, your HR policies, your financial plan, and other "books" that reflect your various areas of expertise and functional responsibility. If these books of yours stand all alone on the top of the bookshelf, they will collect dust and they will most likely fall down or out of alignment without bookends.

Your organization and your team must have bookends. From my experience, the most useful bookends are these: On the left of the books, you will have a strong sense of your *Core Purpose* and on the right of your books you will have a very clear *Customer Focus*. With your purpose in mind and a clear commitment to your customers, you will be guided to do the right thing and you will find that the books on your bookshelf stay in alignment.

Bookends for Life

As with an organization, each individual has written and continues to write the books of his or her life. These books of life benefit from bookends in the same way an organization benefits when these come into alignment. The following illustration is about your personal bookends.

I propose that the bookend on the left, for the books of your life, is your individual sense of a Core Purpose—the "Why-to" for your daily walks of life. This Core Purpose will become the legacy you leave behind and perhaps be represented in words in the eulogy given as you make your life's exit one day. The bookend on the right is "Who you decide to *Be* each day to create that legacy." As a practical way to affirm your commitments to your purpose, I offer this suggestion. Illustrate your Core Purpose (what you would be known for, your legacy) by three words or short phrases that are easy to remember. Pick one word for each of three aspects of your life: *You*, *Your Work*, and *Others*. First pick a word or phrase that describes a key element of your character that you are cultivating, then another that illustrates the essence of your life's work, and finally a third word that conveys your intent as you interact with the people in your life. My examples are these:

✓ You: Power with Purpose.

✓ Work: Helping God, Archimedes, and You to Lift the World.

✓ Others: Quick to Build.

I have not arrived at these. These are ongoing, long-term goals for my life. These are about how I hope my family and friends will remember my contributions and me when I am gone. These are guideposts for my life to reduce the probability that I might arrive at the end and say, "Is that all there is to life?"

As for the right-hand bookend of your life, may I invite you to consider several words or short phrases that would characterize who you intend to *Be* each day to stay on track with the legacy you will create over time. These will be very practical, here-and-now affirmations. You will let these words quickly pass through your mind or you may actually say them out loud each morning between the time your alarm clock rings and no more than five minutes thereafter. These three words or phrases will *Be* the basic mental program that helps you to operate your mind and direct your spiritual energies throughout the day. My three phrases are:

✓ You: Energized and Present.

✓ Work: The Voice of the Cricket. (I will share more about "the cricket" very soon.)

✓ Others: Acknowledge, Acknowledge, Acknowledge.

Your Bookends

What will be the nature of your bookends? These will help you stay aligned and stand firmly as you lift the world. Now, I will tell you the inspirational story of an extraordinary man named Peter Madike from a faraway land called Ikeja. His bookends are clearly, simply, and profoundly *in place*.

The Saga of Peter Madike

At the time when I made my journeys to Lagos, Nigeria, I understood that the city had more than 10 million residents. Approximately 500,000 of these people lived "in the streets" in one manner or another. When I was there, the government was essentially a military dictatorship. This meant that the law was whatever the nearest soldier or policeman decided it would be. As with most major cities in any country, there were wrong places to be at the wrong time that spelled danger. And the absence of reliable law enforcement made things a bit more dicey. This fact, coupled with the hectic manner of driving on the crowded Lagos streets, meant that foreigners were advised not to drive themselves around town. Caleb Yaro's bank graciously provided me with a driver. His name was Peter Madike.

Peter was originally from the eastern part of Nigeria. He is about 5 feet 6 inches tall and weighed around 125 pounds. I guessed that he was around 40 years of age. His wife is Adankwo and they had six children at the time. They all lived together in a poor section of Lagos known as Ikeja.

Peter would catch five different buses and travel for more than two hours, morning and night, to make his way between his home and the bank headquarters. His monthly salary was the equivalent of about $60 (U.S.) He had served the bank faithfully for a number of years. Peter took his two chief responsibilities very seriously: driving the car, and assuring my all-around safety.

There are many stories I can tell of my travels with Peter. He became a marvelous friend. I often acknowledged Peter's helpfulness and special wisdom. Each day, Peter would deliver me from my nighttime compound to the Banker's Institute on Victoria Island, the wealthy section of Lagos. My students from several banks and other organizations would be waiting inside to greet me. I would walk to the front of the auditorium with Peter at my side. He insisted on carrying my bag full of my presentation materials. As he would turn to depart from the auditorium, I would thank him and shake his hand. Then, as the class began, I would often recount some adventure or conversation Peter and I had shared that morning on our way to the Institute.

As you would guess, a "driver" is pretty low in the hierarchy of a bank. Conversely, those of my students who were the bank managers were the elite in the community. Though Nigeria is certainly a "developing" country, these bankers lived in beautiful homes, drove BMWs, and most of them had several household servants. There were two reactions to my public acknowledgment of Peter as my co-equal buddy that took awhile to surface. After several days of training, a group of my bank manager friends approached me and expressed their surprise that I was "hanging out" with my driver. They thought it to be quite a novel thing and I could tell it even made them uncomfortable that I may have crossed some "class barrier" in my friendship with Peter. The other result was that Peter overheard my public acknowledgments and was positively overwhelmed by my public support of his role at the bank.

A Visit to Peter's Home

It was during my second trip to Nigeria that I discovered the true character of my friend, Peter Madike.

As I had become more familiar with the Lagos area, I decided it was time to venture farther outside the central city. I told Peter that I would like to visit his home and meet his family. At first, he seemed a little reluctant. I let a few days go by and he finally brought the subject up himself. We decided to take a Sunday trip to attend a Christian church in his neighborhood and to meet his family.

Our car twisted and turned down one dirt road, then another, and then another. We passed many humble homes and simple shops. We came to a two story building with dozens of children playing in the front yard. It was an apartment building about the size of my current home in Arizona. I learned that it housed 12 families, including Peter's. As I stepped from the car, the most surprising thing I noticed was the open sewage trench that ran along the road about 20 feet in front of the homes. Children were playfully hopping back and forth across the trench. Women were leaning over the edge cleaning fish. Other children were relieving themselves in the ditch and then jumping up to continue their play.

Peter took me inside his apartment home. His beautiful and humble wife, Adankwo, politely greeted me with very timid eye contact. She was holding their youngest child. Five other children came scurrying in from either the back room of the apartment or from the front yard. I can honestly say that what next met my eyes was one of the most cheerful, friendly, polite group of children I've ever met anywhere. Their clothes were somewhat tattered and their feet were bare, but their faces beamed.

Peter and Adankwo showed me inside. Their home consisted of two rooms, each about 10 or 12 feet square. The main room had a small 1960s TV, a small table with an electric cooking device on top, and a very worn sofa with holes clear through to daylight in the center of each cushion. Everything was old and worn, but neatly arranged. In the bedroom was the sagging double bed where Peter, Adankwo, and the baby slept. The three oldest children slept on a mat in the center of the floor. Two younger and smaller children each slept on one of the two shelves hanging from the wall opposite the double bed. These shelves were about 18 inches deep, with an outer railing, and covered with crumpled blankets.

I sat down in the living room for about an hour and visited with Peter and Adankwo. They told me of their village in eastern Nigeria and the great economic problems there. They had left their families and come to the big city so Peter could find work. They longed to return home. I am sure they had almost no way of communicating with the family and friends they had left behind. As the afternoon wore on, Peter and I soon realized we needed to be on our way to get me back across the city to my safe compound before dark. And now comes one of the most profound moments in my relationship with Peter, and perhaps in my entire life.

Peter's First Line of Defense

Peter and I walked out the door, said goodbye to Adankwo and the baby, and then crossed the sewage trench to get in our car and drive off. My first thought was of the smiling faces of Peter's children, and then my thoughts turned to concern. I thought of the sewage trench and how exposed these children were to the elements, to insects, and to germs of all kinds. I turned to Peter and asked, "How do you keep your children so healthy? Do you have a hospital or doctor nearby, Peter? There are so many germs in those ditches that could make children sick."

"Yes," Peter said. "See that white building over there? That is a small hospital if children get very sick."

The conversation continued briefly. "Peter, I realize that our children in the United States are lucky to *not* have so many dangers to their health. I guess I am surprised and happy that your children are so strong and healthy."

Then, Peter turned to me with the most puzzled look on his face and thoughtfully said, "But, Darby, Jesus takes care of my children. I don't worry. I have faith that God will protect them."

I was speechless and could only stare out the front windshield as I struggled to maintain my composure and conceal what was almost a feeling of shame. I am a Christian and consider myself to be a man of faith. And yet, I suddenly realized that my natural inclination might be to first look to doctors and hospitals to protect the health of my children. Then, I would pray and ask God for his tender mercies. Peter's faith was unquestionably his first line of defense. I had come to Nigeria to teach. On this day, I was Peter's student. Peter's bookends were clearly in place. He helped me to reexamine mine.

What are those three words/phrases you will bring to mind when your alarm clock rings tomorrow morning? Who will you be to create the legacy that is yours?

Leverage Key 3

The Five Arenas of Life

City Slickers is one of my favorite movies. Those who have seen the movie will remember the wonderful moment when Jack Palance, playing the hardened ranch foreman, Curly, is riding along with Billy Crystal, who has come to the dude ranch to work through his midlife crisis. As they ride along, Jack Palance cuts Billy Crystal down to size with a combination of cynicism and wisdom. He says something to this effect: "You city dudes, you turn 45 or so, you find you've suddenly got hair growing out of your ears, and your marriage is all messed up. So, you decide to come out here and reinvent your life, right? You want to get in touch with the real world." Billy Crystal says, "Yeah, that's it. Curly, what's the secret?" Then Jack

Palance raises that big index finger, covered with that black leather glove, and says, "It's just one thing." The conversation continues: "Just one thing? What is the one thing?" Jack Palance replies, "You'll know."

It's Just One Thing!

A big factor in successfully navigating through life is to recognize and focus on your true *Priorities*. What is the "one thing"? How will you know? Whether it's one thing or the top three, or this year's list of 10 must-do goals, how will we each know what is most important? Sometimes we get a wake-up call that makes everything real clear. Let me share with you my biggest wake-up call ever. It occurred in December of 2003.

The Wake-Up Call

At this point in my life, our son, Matthew, was serving a mission in Ecuador. He is the youngest of our seven children. He became particularly close to Sharon and me because he was our only experience with an "only child" relationship. His brothers and sisters had all grown up and moved on with their own lives by the time he was 12 years old. At that time, we moved our household and business from Utah to Arizona. For the next seven years, he lived with just his mom and dad. Our relationship became a very meaningful three-way friendship. He was never a troublesome teenager. He could have thought he was stuck living with a couple of 50-something-year-old fogies. Instead, he was so relaxed with us and so respectful.

So, this precious son of mine was in faraway Ecuador. We missed him and yet we were of proud of him and his work. About three months before he was due to come home, I noticed some puzzling physical symptoms: an area of lumpiness in my groin, soon accompanied by significant swelling of my left leg. It turned out that this swelling was a blessing, as I would otherwise have continued to be unaware of what was going on inside my body.

I was soon diagnosed with cancer. After the MRIs and CT scans, on my third visit to the doctor, he said, "You do have lymphoma, but what's causing your leg to swell up is that the enlarged lymph nodes have pinched the inguinal vein in your leg and created a clot that is impeding circulation." I learned that the clot was in a very bad place. It could break and sail up to my heart or lung and kill me in a matter of seconds. The doctor went on to say, "We will immediately put you on blood thinners and watch your progress closely."

The Emotional Bombshell

Sharon and I began to struggle with this emotional bombshell. "Wow, I have cancer. I never expected this. This is life threatening." But the biggest fear was that I could die at any moment from the blood clot. Will it happen in an hour? Will it happen while I'm sleeping tonight? How long will it take for the blood thinners to kick in? Will they dissolve the clot or will it just break up and a piece will go to my lungs anyway?

For only the second time in my life, I realized I could actually die. The earlier realization had been a situational one that passed quickly. This time, the threat to my life was far more complex and would be far more difficult to resolve. My mortality was an instant reality. With just a little contemplation of my situation, my greatest personal apprehensions and sadness rose to the surface. I love my wife and cherish her companionship. At the same time, I knew that if something happened to me, she would go on with her life. Our children would rally around her. But what about Matt? As I thought about my youngest son, I said to Sharon, "I want him home. As positive as I tried to be, I would just feel cheated in life if I couldn't hold him in my arms and welcome him back from his two years of wonderful service to the people of Ecuador." And so I would get on my knees and pray.

An Angel from South Carolina

I had recently formed a new friendship with a devout Christian gentleman from South Carolina, Dr. Roger Roff. We had e-mailed each other periodically about our business ventures and various community service projects. When he learned of my cancer diagnosis, he was stunned. He knew what a healthy man I had been and he knew the vigor with which I approached life. In an instant, he became an angel sent to comfort me and buoy me up at this crucial moment in my life. He sent me a most remarkable, life-changing e-mail. I share it with you here exactly as he wrote it.

Dear Darby...

First: God bless you and may God sustain you. My second thought: God seldom strikes down someone that has an enormous project that Glorifies God and perpetuates the betterment of mankind.

You do this daily. My third thought is: God often puts his select disciples to test so that the disciple might grow and become mightier in HIS service because of deeper insights and spiritual understandings. I know for an absolute certainty that whatever the threat, the overall victory for you, your family, or the world will be spectacular. It's just going through the process that is so burdensome, lonely, and anguishing.

Do not take ownership of the lymphoma only. Own the wholeness and the beauty of the magnificence of the perfect body God has given you. That does not mean you deny there is an invader, but you hire someone to capture, arrest, and remove the unwanted invader from your body. The invader-hunter is God and your oncologist.

You must now elevate your consciousness to a higher level through thoughts, singing, listening to joyful music, being with fine friends, relishing the moments with your wife and family, and encourage the manufacture of the brain's endorphins to go out of control as you stay in a euphoric state of conscious thankfulness and joy. Elevation of consciousness is an extremely powerful tool for the improvement of all bodily functions and the ridding of anything undesirable. The big secret is: Own only that which is perfect for bodily function.

I was buoyed up by the profound faith and the positive energy of this great man and his message. I was also humbled, as I did not feel worthy of his opening lines. All that I believed and had taught others would now be put to the test. This cancer invader would test my will and my faith. I decided that, above all, this would be a profound learning experience. I realized that my grandchildren would be watching their grandfather and learning from him how to handle adversity.

Please, Let Your Son Bless My Son

Then, there was Matt. The way I was able to deal with my longing to see Matt was this. Hanging on one wall of my office is a picture of Jesus Christ stepping out of the tomb. On an adjacent wall is a photograph of my three younger sons and me river rafting in Colorado. Sitting in the front of the raft is Matthew. As I would pray for protection and strength, I would go to the picture of Christ and touch his hand and then go to the other picture and touch the face of Matt. I would plead, "Heavenly Father, you understand about sons. Please let your son bless my son and me that we will be reunited before I'm called home." So, I followed a simple ritual in my office. I would touch the hand of Christ and touch the face of Matt. My faith sustained me. My resolve to fight cancer and win was strengthened. God heard my plea.

I have never felt my heart so full as when Matt got off the plane at Sky Harbor airport in Phoenix, Arizona. I was still alive. He came to me. We put our heads on each other's shoulders and sobbed together while Sharon stood by.

Life Is More Precious When There Is Less of It to Live

My priorities are clearer than they have ever been before. I even know the "one thing" about which that old ranch foreman spoke of when he admonished Billy Crystal. During the early days of my encounter with cancer, I created in my planner a list of eight events and accomplishments that prompted this conversation with God. I said, "God, I've had a great life. If I died I wouldn't be the first guy to die at 59. I really couldn't complain. Plenty of young men have been in a car accident at 26 and left their bride and two kids and didn't get to live past that young age. There are American, Iraqi, and Afghan soldiers and civilians losing their lives daily, getting blown up by roadside bombs and leaving their families behind. So, I'm lucky, God, I've made it to 59 years. I can die and I won't be angry and I won't be bitter. I would like to see my son. Also, God, I have written down eight things in my planner that, if possible, I would ask for maybe a little extra time and help to do these eight things before I go home."

These eight items have all been completed. I have been blessed. New, high-priority goals have extended the list and I am hard at work on these, including the creation of this book. I now regularly recall the words of Bonnie Raitt's song, "Life is more precious when there's less of it to live." My priorities are very clear. The trivia of life doesn't get in the way as much. As I conclude the account of this amazing learning experience, I must give credit to God, to my dear wife, to Dr. Roff, to many dear friends, to my precious children, and to the skillful and caring medical staff of the Mayo Clinic in Scottsdale, Arizona. My invader-hunters were God, with his healing power, and my oncologist, Dr. Michael Gornet.

The Five Arenas of Life

In some of my seminars, when I help my friends strengthen their determination to set goals and be clear about their priorities, I share this illustration and engage them in the discussion and thoughtful examination of the Five Arenas of Life.

Family/ Friends	Community	Career	Self	(Other)
✓	✓	✓	✓	✓
✓	✓	✓	✓	✓
✓	✓	✓	✓	✓
✓	✓	✓	✓	✓
✓	✓	✓	✓	✓
✓	✓	✓	✓	✓
✓	✓	✓	✓	✓
✓	✓	✓	✓	✓

I propose to my seminar audiences (and to you) that there are at least five major arenas of life that most of us have in common. The fifth arena, I call "Other" and leave it to the audience members to label it as their church, special spiritual commitment, perhaps a professional organization of unusual importance, or possibly a cherished hobby. I then pose this question: Which of these five arenas is "number one"? It is amazing how little time it takes for real controversy to emerge. Someone in the audience speaks up and says, "Well, for heaven's sake, your family is number one. That's the most important thing for any of us in this world, family."

And then someone else says, "No, no, no. Of what use would you be to your family if you weren't in good health and you hadn't taken care of yourself? You've got to put 'number one' as number one, which is yourself." And then someone else raises their hand and says, "Career is really where most people find their sense of self-worth. Your professional commitments are who you are." Often, someone will bravely speak up and say, "Well, what about the Kingdom of God? Isn't that most important of all?"

Which Is Number One?

So we get this great debate going and then I say, "All right. Thank you for all those wonderful thoughts; those are powerful thoughts. I'm going to be so bold now as to presume to tell you which of these is number one." And everybody waits in suspense. Then I click my little PowerPoint clicker and I say, "Family is number one. Community is number one. Career is number one. Self is number one. Your 'Other' category that is so important to you is number one. And God cares about all five arenas of your life. Imagine going to your boss at work and saying, 'I told my wife and children that I'm going to be an absolute first-rate father. This means I've sort of got to be a second-rate, second-level engineer. I hope you understand.' Or imagine going home to your wife and saying, 'Honey, I promised my boss I'd be the best engineer on the team, but that means I'm going to have to be a second-tier father. You understand, right?'" I continue my presentation: "Ladies and gentlemen, you couldn't sell such a 'second-rate' commitment in either of these situations, could you?"

The bottom line is that you want a level of excellence in every one of these Five Arenas of Life. The issue is what's underneath the five column headings, the long to-do lists. You may have six or seven things in the next week under Family and four or five commitments to your community. You've got all sorts of projects at work, PowerPoint presentations to design and Excel spreadsheets to create, and so many meetings to attend. And then you've got *you* to worry about. You've got to exercise daily. You've got to read that new book you just heard about. You've got all this stuff. And I'll even bet somebody out there in the audience somewhere is driving himself a little crazy at this moment because, guess what he's got in his wallet? A $5-off Jiffy Lube coupon. And that $5-off coupon expires at the end of the month. Your priorities are being influenced by a $5 coupon. Throw it away. Life is too precious to be driven by a coupon of any kind. The problem is the prioritizing you need to do in each of those checklists under each of the Five Arenas of Life."

Playing the five arenas off against each other is a great fallacy. Again, you and I want a level of excellence in every one of these great arenas. The secret is to be present for the things that count and make a difference in each arena. I call it "Wherever you are, be there." Most people are relieved to know that all five arenas are number one and that it's the prioritizing of activities under each column that is the issue. Get rid of the trivia in each column. Know what is "number one" in each column. The great message is this: Of the 5, 7, or 10 items on the to-do list in each arena of your life, which ones would you do if you had cancer and were not sure how long you had to live? You would decide that life is suddenly too precious to try and do everything and certainly too precious to do the trivia that so easily gets heaped on the platters of our lives.

Did I Do the Thing That Counted Most?

Ask yourself at the end of each day this simple series of questions: "Did I do the thing that counted most with my 15-year-old today...that counted most for our community...that counted most at work...that counted most for my own good health and well being...that counted most for God?" And isn't it interesting as you count the "one thing"? The one thing is that you are committed to excellence in all the important things you do, which means that you do what counts most. You have the courage and the presence of mind to put other things aside that would detract from the true priorities that represent genuine success and true happiness for you, for those you love, and for those who count on you. Knowing your priorities is to have very, very important leverage on your time—your precious time.

Leverage Key 4

Listen for the Voice
of the Cricket

To understand the world you intend to lift, you must be able to hear the world. Perhaps you will hear it whisper, chuckle, sigh, shout with joy, or moan. To learn how to *hear* the world, learn to *listen* for the voice of the cricket.

The Fabulous Ray Charles

Have you seen and experienced the movie *Ray*? It is the story of the fabulous Ray Charles. As the movie and his childhood begins, your heartstrings will be pulled and you'll soon find your foot tapping to the amazing rhythms this genius could create. Soon, you will be reminded that even those with great gifts and incredible potential can get so far off track and bring about so much heartache and tragedy. The hell Ray Charles eventually goes through could be characterized by another "h" word. "Oh yes, heroin," you recall. You're right, heroin. Thankfully, our hero, Ray, was rescued from his downfall. He was saved in the end by the voice of the cricket.

If you have not seen the movie *Ray*, I hope it will soon be on your must-see list. I promise that as you listen with your heart to one particular segment of the movie, you will mark it down in your memory as one of the most truly tender moments in movie history. In this one special scene, you will see profound love and a lifetime of parenting wisdom unfold in just minutes.

Profound Love...a Lifetime of Wisdom

It was much to my surprise that I learned Ray was not born blind. He began gradually going blind at age 7. Doctors were at a loss to understand and to treat this malady that came about with such surprise and sadness. As a measure of hope, Ray's mother would put salve on his eyes. One afternoon, she was working in the back room of the very humble, two-room home she shared with her sons. Up the front steps came little Ray, feeling his way, salve in his eyes. As he stepped inside the front door, he walked just two more steps until he hit the edge of the rug, tripped, and fell flat on his face. He began to cry and called out for his mother. Then, he leaned up on his elbows and moved his head from side to side, attempting to see or sense who was in the house, hoping for help to come. And where was his mother?

Ray's mother stood silently in the other corner of the room. She watched him fall and begin to cry. She took a tentative step forward, wanting to reach out and pick him up. And then, for some reason, she caught herself, stood back, and stayed very quiet. She watched. She had realized that this was to be one of the most significant moments in her son's entire life.

Soon Ray stopped crying, sobbed softly, carefully got up and dusted himself off. At that instant, a horse-drawn wagon came down the street, passing near the front steps of the house. He cocked his head and studied the sound of horses' hooves. Then Ray walked a few short steps further into the house. He moved to the right. He heard the soft chirping of a cricket (or small grasshopper). His mother watched from the corner of the room. The sound of the cricket moved. Ray followed with his ears. It was now nearby under a chair. Ray knelt down, inched his way toward the sound of the cricket, and slid his hand slowly across the floor. All he knew was the sound. He reached under the chair, carefully felt around until he grabbed the little cricket and held it up to his ear. His mother had tip toed just a little closer and was now a few feet away from her son. He could not see her. She stood still. Very slowly, he moved his head upward in her direction. Holding the cricket in his hand, he said, "Mama, you're there, aren't you?"

Ray had sensed her presence. Perhaps he could hear her softly breathing. He hadn't heard his mother breathing until he had first listened for the cricket. Now, his mother reached out to him. Through her patience, he had been allowed to learn what no one could ever teach him: he could find his own way. And even though he had to learn this on his own, she was there for him. Not to do it for him, but to be there as he did it.

Is Anyone Coming? Am I Enough?

Steve Chandler is my great friend and mentor. He represents to me what I refer to as a "cascade of coaching" or a "cascade of wisdom." This is the benefit that comes from being coached by someone who is coached by someone who has learned from others who possess great wisdom. It was Steve who originally shared this particularly powerful life lesson with me: No one is coming.

Steve teaches what he refers to as the "Ownership Spirit." In his books and seminars, he explains that as we each grow and mature, there comes a time when we discover the ultimate spirit of ownership. We realize we must develop the inner strength to accept the fact that "it is up to me." If I face a difficult situation and no one comes to my aid, I will be enough. This realization comes to a child that first time she falls, scrapes her knee, cries, hopes that her mother or father will come, and they do not. When no one comes, she picks herself up, dusts herself off, and proceeds on her way. At that moment, the little child has taken a giant step forward in growing up and learning to take responsibility for her life. She has tasted the ownership spirit.

Ray's mother realized that Ray needed to experience his fall to the floor without help from outside. He had to find the strength within to find his way. As I have pondered the wisdom Steve Chandler helped me crystallize with "no one is coming," the story of Ray added a marvelous new corollary. The expanded wisdom is that "no one is coming, but someone is there."

Ray's mother had the intuition to realize that she had to let Ray find his way, but she was there nevertheless watching over him. Sometimes in life, no one is coming, but we sense that someone is there. At different times, in different ways, we will each discover who is silently but powerfully there for us. Later in Ray's life, the voice of the cricket, the sound of his mother softly breathing, and the power of her great love returned to rescue him from the hell that could have consumed him.

There is leverage for life in the voice of the cricket. We must listen to the voice of the cricket to hear the world whisper, chuckle, sigh, shout with joy, or moan. And as we hear what the world is saying, we are better prepared to lift the world. Listen to your world. Listen to everything and everyone in it. You will hear what it wants you to know.

Leverage Key 5

Who in the World
Is Out There?

With the right leverage, you will rock and lift your own world and the worlds of others. Who do you have in mind? Will these others be your family, your work associates, your community, or humanity in general? As we reflect on those with whom we share the planet, we soon recognize the amazing interconnectedness that exists among us. There is often a surprising and powerful ripple effect of one person's actions on numerous others out there somewhere. We have heard of the principle of "six degrees of separation," which is that any one person is probably only six key contacts away from any other person on the planet. With all this in mind and based on your dreams and ambitions, begin to imagine who you might influence or help as you gain the leverage of Archimedes. Please consider this modern parable as a place to begin.

A Pilgrimage to Costco

When my wife, Sharon, and I make our semi-monthly pilgrimage to Costco, one of the prime items on our shopping list is a jar of Kirkland/Signature Cashews. They are the plumpest, most tender-crunchy cashews of the most consistent quality we have ever enjoyed. I have consumed so many handfuls of these delectable nuts over the past several years. It may seem a little strange, but the cashew jar label stirs a certain emotion in me. I truly do not take these wonderful nuts or their ultimate source for granted.

The Appreciation Factor

Somewhere in my development, I acquired what I call an "appreciation factor." I rarely take for granted the many and varied contributions of those around me, or even the contributions of those far away who are somehow connected with something that makes my life better. I am one of those rare guys who thanks the janitor in the men's room at the airport. Please don't misconstrue this appreciation factor as a noble thing. I don't serve in a food kitchen for the homeless. I'm not without selfishness. Perhaps my willingness to at least acknowledge others is a result of my mother's unconditional love. Perhaps it is about my father's generosity. I think it is somehow mystically tied to the unique boyhood experience of working at the side of a humble Navajo man named Donald.

Donald was employed by my father to help care for our small ranch in South Phoenix, Arizona. From the age of 10 to 16 years, I worked with Donald throughout the school year on Saturdays, and several days a week during the summer months. He was in his early 40s. His life on the reservation had been very hard. He had taken up drinking and constantly apologized for that fact, and for the effects on his family. Donald was a hard worker and a good friend. I knew that when he listened to me, he really listened. He did not judge. He was curious. He supported my thinking as I recounted to him the frustrations of a teenage boy. My heart was touched as he unfairly criticized himself. I was quick to see the good in him and to reassure him. This friendship had an important influence on me. Friendship is leverage on the quality of our lives. It begins with basic appreciation and acknowledgement of others...of their trials, their courage, their fundamental goodness, and the work they do for others.

Fancy Whole Indian Cashews

About the third time I held a jar of Costco's Kirkland brand cashews in my hand, I noticed the phrase "Fancy Whole Indian Cashews" on the label. I immediately envisioned the plantations of India portrayed on National Geographic specials with poorly-clad, brown-skinned workers moving through the groves of nut trees, checking the plant leaves for insects, inspecting the nutshells for size and shape, then ultimately harvesting (however you harvest) cashew nuts and placing them in large wooden crates to be shipped to the nearby village. There the nuts would be sorted, shelled, dried, and packed for shipping. I imagined an Indian plantation worker taking pride in his or her crop. I also imagined payday with just a few coins being placed in a rough, brown hand that had tended the plants and endured the relentless beating of the sun.

Costco sells many, many jars of cashew nuts and reaps significant profits from these, I'm sure. Costco stockholders benefit. Their wealth sends their children to college and provides the funds for other business enterprises that create jobs in my hometown, in your hometown, and probably as far away as Hong Kong. There are cashew nut processors, warehouse operators, brokers, and nut transporters who make a good business from these nuts. Ultimately Costco customers benefit from a quality product at a very fair price due principally to three factors, I believe: (a) Costco's volume purchasing power, (b) various processing efficiencies, and (c) inexpensive plantation labor.

I appreciate Costco's genius. They have a great deal of leverage in the world. That leverage creates a chain of events that nurtures a "chain of customers" that helps to make the world go 'round. My concern is that we somehow not forget to acknowledge that plantation worker who first picked the cashew nuts and for whom that modest wage provides a basic requirement of food and clothing for his children.

How Will You Rock the World?

Costco's leverage rocks the world all the way to the dinner table in a rural village in India. I wonder how many Costco shoppers really notice the word "Indian" on their cashew nut jar. Does it matter that they do or don't? Does it matter that I do?

What is the leverage of your work, of your friendships, of your own business enterprise? How will you rock the world and lift the world by what you do? Will you build a Costco empire? Will you provide jobs for plantation workers? Will you befriend a "Donald" who, in turn, blesses your life? Will you change? Will your children see your generosity and change? Do not under-estimate the cause and effect relationship of who you are and what you do that lifts the worlds of those around you.

Guy Kawasaki once said, "You can be rich, you can be powerful, and you can be famous, but you won't amount to much of anything until you change the world."

Mr. Kawasaki's statement is meant to be inspiring and not intimidating, for it is not difficult to change the world. Who you are and what you do makes a difference, large or small. The amazing Costco empire provides me with cashews. Donald, my boyhood friend, changed my life by simply listening.

Leverage Key 6

Vision: Demystify It and Go There!

Our worst fear is not that we are inadequate. Our deepest fear is that we are powerful beyond measure. It is our light, not our darkness, that most frightens us. We ask ourselves, "Who am I to be brilliant, gorgeous, talented and fabulous?" Actually, who are you not to be?

—Marianne Williamson

Prepare to close your eyes. As you do, and in your mind's eye, you will see the reverse images of the light and dark objects you had just seen with your eyes wide open. Now that you've opened your eyes, prepare to close them again. This time, picture the steepest section of a roller coaster with the cars just beginning their descent and people holding their arms high in the air. Close your eyes again to recall a photograph of yourself as a 3- or 4-year-old and see yourself running across a patch of bright, green grass and into the camera lens. Next, transport yourself mentally to the plains of Africa to see a giraffe galloping with its neck swaying forward and back. Imagine yourself on a mountain peak rotating 360 degrees to see a panorama of clouds, valleys, lakes, and other mountain peaks in the distance.

Finally, close your eyes one more time and picture yourself being interviewed by Larry King. Why are you being interviewed? Your new book has become a blockbuster success. Your company is the leading manufacturer of accessories for the iPod and your sales team launched the latest breakthrough product that is taking the world by storm. You have just led a team of adventurers across a previously unexplored glacier in Antarctica. Your family has been chosen by the local mayor's office to lead the Fourth of July parade. You are being recognized as an "All American Family."

You Can't Shrink Your Way to Greatness

Tom Peters once said, "You can't shrink your way to greatness." You must see B-I-G. You must be able to see your success and your visionary accomplishments in your mind's eye or these will never happen. Imagination is a magnetic force that draws all the molecules of your body into a creative force for change. Some may think the idea of vision is reserved for geniuses, prophets, and heroes. It depends on whom the vision is intended to benefit. If you expect your vision to influence the destinies of nations or to unite the human race, you may be waiting for that rare moment in history in which you may play a part. On the other hand, if you expect your vision to set in motion a chain of events that will change the future for your family, your company, or your community, you are entitled to dream big and to have inspiration pour in from many sources to help your vision become reality.

If you intend to change the world, you must see BIG or you will not see enough. A great vision is propelled into its powerful existence by two things: (1) a "Kevlar thread" of purpose that runs through your life and lifts your spirit; (2) a particularly aggressive performance goal. This goal must be big enough to demand that you think beyond your own capabilities to form powerful partnerships that you would otherwise have not considered. Take into consideration what W.H. Murray once said:

> *Until one is committed there is hesitancy, the chance to draw back, always ineffectiveness. Concerning all acts of initiative (and creation), there is one elementary truth, the ignorance of which kills countless ideas and splendid plans; that the moment one definitely commits oneself, then providence moves too. All sorts of things occur to help one that would never otherwise have occurred. A whole stream of events issue from the decision, raising in one's favor all manner of unforeseen incidents and meetings and material assistance which no man (or woman) could have dreamt would have come his way.*

Vision Is Not Mystical

Vision is not mystical. Vision is simply bringing *high purpose* together with *daring goals* to ultimately form a "picture of doneness" that you can see in your mind's eye. Then, you decide to go there! You march forward with constant decisiveness. You organize your daily thoughts to center on the vision. You marshal resources. You ignore pessimists. You do not look back. You see the finish line. And you may even choose to see yourself face to face with Larry King. Don't stop until you get there. To assure victory, examine these once again:

1. Is your thread of purpose strong and invulnerable?

2. Is your goal BIG enough to inspire others and to win their dedication? Big is defined not as outlandish or extreme, but on the basis of "Is it worth the effort?" This means that the impact of achieving the goal will be immensely satisfying, rewarding, and beneficial.

3. Last but not least, can you close your eyes and see it?

You're In the News!

Write it down...all of it. In written or typed words, describe your purpose and what it is inside you, what it is about your life's experience that brought you to this sense of purpose. List the major actions required to achieve the goal and for each action identify what will be satisfying, rewarding, and beneficial about that action item as a milestone on the way to turning your vision into reality. Finally, become the reporter who is interviewing you for a national magazine. You and your partners have succeeded and the world wants to know about it. Write a synopsis of the article to vividly describe your triumph and the difference it has made. Describe your feelings of exhilaration as you realized "we've done it" and as you hugged your partners and thanked them for making the impossible achievable. *Go there! Be there!* Write this story as if it has happened and your subconscious mind will help you make it so. Read it again and again, day by day.

Hello, Archimedes...Are you there?

Is vision leverage? Ancient scriptures tell us that without it "the people perish." Vision is more than leverage; it is *The Force*. It is the force for everything significant that has ever happened on the planet. Could Washington see himself on the other side of the Delaware? Would it be worth it to go there? Could Edison see himself seeing in the dark aided by a glowing lamp without a flickering flame and the odor of kerosene? Would it be worth it to experiment, experiment, and experiment a thousand times? Could your high school math teacher envision you receiving your college diploma? Would it be worth it? What would you like to change, achieve, improve, or contribute that will be worth the effort? Go there!

Leverage Key 7

Principle-Centered: Do the Right Thing

I've always understood that "doing it right" is being *efficient*. "Doing the right it" is being *effective*. It's great to be both effective and efficient. However, there's one thing greater than "doing the right it." It is doing something that is anchored in purpose and principle and which has an unquestionably positive impact on all who are involved. For many years in operating my consulting business, I have been known for promoting service excellence through a series of programs and products labeled "Customer Astonishment." As part of this family of products, our company created a professional certification process whereby the candidate qualifies as a "Customer Champion." The following is the definition of a "Customer Champion" that guides this powerful program. The value of the definition transcends our certification program and contains many elements that are guidelines for true professionalism wherever it is to be found.

A True Customer Champion is defined as: *An individual who works with a clear sense of purpose to satisfy the needs and exceed the expectations of his or her customers. As a true professional, this individual performs to recognized standards of excellence and puts the needs of his/her external and internal customers first in order to produce results that are mutually beneficial.*

Look for the key words in this definition: *purpose, true professional, recognized standards, mutually beneficial.* If we each tried to do what we do with purpose and professionalism while working to clear standards of performance in a way that is mutually beneficial to all who are involved, we'd be really rocking the world in a way that makes a difference.

Do the Right Thing

One of our greatest clients (the company has since expanded, merged, and been sold to a larger corporation) was famous in our book of life for the way each field manager began every team meeting. The opening of the meeting would always include two things: (1) a "safety minute" to help safeguard the lives and limbs of employees and (2) a discussion of their field-operations motto, which was "Do the right thing." The team would take a few minutes to reflect on what "right thing" meant and then share examples where employees had deliberately adjusted their approaches each to other (as internal customers) and to their external customers to be sure everybody would "be right" with the result. This was/is being principle-centered.

Many philosophers, management experts, spiritual leaders, and others have taught about being "principle-centered." It sounds good but it is not easy. Why? The answer: most of us are somewhat "self-centered." Let me clarify. Self-centered is different from selfish. Selfish implies a me-me gratification need. Self-centered means that I'm so busy focusing on all the "stuff" in my life that I have to remember to look up from my desk to remember there are others out there depending on me to do the right thing. Inadvertently, doing the right thing may become "doing what I think I need to do to just get through the day, to minimize my own stress, and to be sure my fundamental needs are met." Perhaps this has to do with that famous "Maslow's Hierarchy of Needs." Until I take care of "my basic stuff," it's tough to find time and energy to focus on that "higher level" and seemingly "lofty" stuff that I "oughta do."

Make the Decision—Once!

Okay, here's the key. Being principle-centered does NOT mean two things: (1) It does not mean that you are a Mother Teresa understudy and (2) It does not mean that you have some extra-big action items to add to your to-do list. What it does mean is that there is a "flavor of certainty" to the important things you do as a normal citizen of the planet who is trying each day to be the best version of who you are. The secret to being principle-centered is about two things: (1) You have benefited from being taught, or having read, or somehow having learned various principles upon which success and happiness are based. (2) You make certain decisions about your current and future behaviors once. For instance, someone who learns that people have "property rights" and that it is not good to steal decides once and for all not to be a thief. Therefore, they are not arbitrary about their code of conduct when it comes to stealing. They do not stand in a jewelry store thinking that maybe the pay-off from taking a diamond ring would be worth the risk. They have already made the decision to not steal. Done. They now actually save time by not having to agonize and decide in each and every tempting situation whether to steal or not. It's done. This person is principle-centered about not stealing and respecting the property of others.

Study Your Heroes

If becoming principle-centered is in any way a struggle, get counsel from those wiser than yourself. Pick up some great books. Study the lives of your heroes. Perhaps you are already guided by sound principles that your parents or other trusted mentors taught you, however, you have new responsibilities that demand new behaviors and new commitments. For instance, you learned long ago *to respect the property of others*, but as a new manager, you must learn to *respect the opinions of others* in new ways and more consistently. A key principle may be this: *There is no such thing as a "dumb" idea, only an idea I don't understand at first.* Write down a core set of principles that make sense to you at this stage of your life and given the responsibilities that are yours. Then, for each of the key principles you wrote down, ask yourself: (1) What behaviors will this principle influence, directly and indirectly? (2) Am I prepared to decide *once* and for all to be guided by this principle, without vacillating each time I am faced with a choice? You will now be principle-centered in that dimension of your behavior. As a new manager, when an employee brings you a new idea, you will listen for understanding before you judge the idea.

Firm or Rigid?

The question may be asked, "Is someone who is principle-centered rigid and dogmatic?" You or I could become dogmatic in the eyes of others if we become fanatical about our principles and attempt to preach and impose these principles on others. Rigid is a close cousin to "firm," but not the same. Firm means that you are unwavering in your commitments and yet open to learn and reevaluate changing circumstances. Rigid ultimately means that, as a tree blowing in the wind, you'd rather break than learn to bend with the wind. Bending with the wind is not the same as bowing to the wind. You are flexible. You know when and how far to bend without compromising your underlying principles.

A Boyhood Hero

One of my principle-centered heroes was my high school math teacher, George Anderson. I took his algebra, geometry, and trigonometry classes. He taught the principles of mathematics and lived by three other principles that were obvious to me. He was guided by principles of honesty, discipline, and an unshakeable belief in the potential of each student who entered his classroom. We instinctively knew that he had zero tolerance for any cheating or cutting corners. He expected diligence in all the assignments he gave us. His classroom was a place not of frivolity but of learning. After class, he was a friend. During class, his goal was to empower our futures by helping us make friends with math. He managed to mix friendliness with firmness in a way that caused his students to truly trust him. With Mr. Anderson, we always knew where he stood on matters of honesty and discipline. And we always knew he would stand by us when needed. Archimedes would approve. Mr. Anderson always had a place to stand as he lifted the world. This is what *Purpose* and *Principles* represent: *your place to stand in the world.*

Leverage Key 8

━━━━━ ███████████████ ━━━━━

Fuel Desire, Passion, and Determination

Those who dream by night in the dusty recesses of their minds wake in the day to find that all was vanity; but the dreamers of the day are dangerous people, for they may act their dream with open eyes, and make it possible.

—T. E. Lawrence

My favorite movies about great leaders and their impact on the world are these: *Henry V* with Kenneth Branagh, *Gandhi* with Ben Kingsley, and *Lawrence of Arabia* with Peter O'Toole. Henry V was the all-around inspirational leader. Gandhi was the all-around example of inner strength and profound wisdom. T.E. Lawrence was the epitome of passion. In each case, their great accomplishments were fueled by intense desire that often manifested itself as passion that further fueled the determination each leader needed to change the world. When these driving forces become crystallized and focused, the result is *Vision*, which we previously explored as *The Force*. The beginning of the chapter displays one of my favorite leadership quotes. To some, it is slightly controversial and perhaps intimidating. To others, it is exciting and empowering. What I want you to get from this statement is the *Energy* inside it.

What Do You Want?

Desire is the beginning of it all. What do you *want*? What people *Need* is substantive and is the logical basis for "doing the right thing" and serving others well. But what people *want* is where it all begins, even if what someone wants has little to do with what he or she actually needs. Be aware of *wants*. Heed *wants*. Include *wants*. Identify and harness the energy *wants* represent. What do you want?

When I built my first 150 List, I included the climbing of mountains as the inspiration for also getting something I knew I needed: exercise and fresh air. What I really wanted was to climb mountains with my children as a shared adventure—and without huffing and puffing as "the old guy." Thus, my exercise routines had a purpose, fueled by desire. This is in contrast to exercising because your doctor recommended it or a university study proved that you live 3.7 years longer or because a nagging (sorry, concerned) sister gave you one big guilt trip about your sedentary lifestyle.

Fuel your commitment to exercise with desire. What do you *want* your exercise to help you do or to get?

Of course, after the excitement of wanting something subsides just a little, we usually try to examine whether the want is good for us or not. This makes sense, but knowing what you want is, in itself, a good thing. This wanting force is the *Desire* that fuels your drive and ambition. And guess what? If you are working to be principle-centered (see Leverage Key 7), you already have one sensible, balancing force in place to help you be sure your wants and desires don't cause you to do something too far-fetched, dangerous, or irresponsible.

The Kindling for Passion

You must have desire to have the kindling for passion. Passion will lead to determination. This determination will drive your vision. I hope this is making sense. Now, here comes the fun part. Are you ready? Those individuals, who have firm footing in working to gain leverage on their dreams and goals, do know what they want. List your desires and wants in response to these questions. Add four or five more questions of your own.

1. What do you want to feel like when faced with physically demanding work or the opportunity for adventure?

2. How do you want to look when you walk through a door and others form their first impression of you?

3. If you had plenty of money, what would you want to buy? Where would you want to travel?

What adventure do you want to enjoy with special friends or family?

4. How much money and wealth do you want? Be specific.

5. Who do you want to meet someday soon—a hero, a celebrity, or a long-lost friend?

6. What do you want to learn? Or put it this way, what are a couple of things you are really curious about and want to figure out?

7. What do you want to be "good at?" This is about skills, competencies, talents, athletic ability, crafts and hobbies.

8. What do you want to believe about the purpose and meaning of life?

9. Who do you want to spend more time with?

10. Who do you want to help?

11. Who do you want to remember you later in life?

12. What do you want them to remember about you?

13. What do you want the world to know about who you really are and what you could really accomplish if you could just "let it all out" and be the best, most creative, most powerful version of who you are?

14. What do you want to change about the world that will make it a better place for those you love and for everybody else on the planet?

15. What do you want more than anything else in the world?

16. Do you really want to succeed? Why?

Get the Music Out!

So what are you doing about these wants? Are you just fantasizing? Are you dreaming? Do you have a goal in any of the 16 areas? Are any of the 16 items more important to you than others? Which ones? Circle these. Now, start your 150 List with these. The next Leverage Key will help you set goals in these areas and prepare you to turn *what you want* into *what you get from life*. Otherwise, you are just plodding and wandering through life and will one day ask that question the great Peggy Lee posed in her classic song "Is That All There Is?" Life will pass you by, as they say.

One of the saddest truths of human existence is that many people go to their graves with their music still in them. Get it out. Do something. Turn wants into positive passion coupled with practical determination to get on with getting on. Fuel your goals with strong desire. Live life with zest and with gusto. Have a blast. Include others. Life does go by fast so soak it up. And rely on your core principles and values to guide you to do some good along the way. In the final analysis, *you will GET from life what you GIVE to life and to those with whom you share it.*

As you embark on getting your music out, consider this. What answer will you get if you ask a 5 year old, "Are you good at poetry...at dancing...at singing...at art?" For a majority of children, the response will be yes, yes, yes, yes I am. How can a 5 year old be good at so many cool things? Conversely, you ask a 25 year old the same questions and you hear this, "No, not poetry...dancing, sort of, but I'm embarrassed when others watch me dance...singing, no way...art, maybe Clipart, but that's it." What happened in the 20 years between 5 and 25? Whoops! Some folks buried their music.

As I sit here reflecting on those I know who got their music out, these individuals come to mind:

- ✓ **Pat Tillman.** I'm a resident of Arizona. He's a local hero. As a powerful athlete with a multi-million dollar NFL career on the horizon, he decided to follow in the footsteps of his grandfather, become an Army Ranger, and put his life on the line for his country. Pat Tillman ultimately gave his life in defending our freedom and that of the Afghan people as well. Sometimes desire is having the "guts" to do what you believe you were meant to do, whatever the sacrifices may be.

- ✓ **Ben Hicks.** Ben is my grandson. His dad recently bought us fantastic near-left-field tickets to a Colorado Rockies/St. Louis Cardinals baseball game. Ben took his ball glove and sat ready to catch the first foul ball. That's what he wanted to do. That's what he was determined to do. Foul balls were not forthcoming, but one field hand who strolled past Ben with a couple of practice balls in his hands could not resist the sight of a 9-year-old poised on the edge of his seat with his glove raised just slightly. Ben got his ball. Sometimes you've got to put yourself in the path of opportunity to get what you want.

- ✓ **Elavie Ndura.** She wanted an education. In her native land of Burundi, her school was 200 miles away. She would walk to and from the school each year and sometimes more than once. Her family became victims of political upheaval and violence. She wanted freedom and a bright future for her children. She found her way to the United States where she attended Northern Arizona University and obtained her doctorate in education. We knew her as the gifted French teacher at our son's junior high school and as a devout Christian who wanted to serve God. Her music is way outside her. It lifts everybody around her.

✓ **Donald Trump.** I don't know the guy and I don't like his hair. But you've got to admit, he knows what he wants and he knows how to get it. I am willing to take lessons from The Donald. There's an old saying, "You can't argue with success, even if you don't like the guy's hair." What Mr. Trump does is dare to want it and believe he'll get it.

✓ **Mary Lou Retton.** Do you remember her energy? She said, "Heat is required to forge anything. Every great accomplishment is the story of a flaming heart." At 4 feet 8 inches and 94 pounds, she won our hearts and won a place in history. Describing her success she went on to say, "I'm very determined and stubborn. There's a *desire* in me that makes me want to do more and more, and to do it right." She was the first American to win the gold medal in the All-Around in women's gymnastics because she wanted to bad enough.

What do you want? Desire is leverage!

Leverage Key 9

What Must I Give
to Succeed?

Imagine yourself at a NASCAR event with your favorite driver zooming around the track. You've probably heard the words, "Go, baby, go!" We cheer our heroes on to victory. As I recall having encouraged a family member or friend in a bicycle or other race with the same words, the thought comes to mind that in the race of life, it's about "Grow, baby, grow." We start as babies and we do grow. The challenge is to keep on growing.

Human potential is limitless. If you doubt it, consider this: Can your brain ever fill up and have no room for a single new tidbit of information? Even the 97-year-old with a couple of Ph.D.s can still learn a new fact or contemplate a new thought. Imagine the converse. What if your brain had a limit as to how many new world cultures you could possibly contemplate in a lifetime? For instance, you're scheduling your seventh global vacation and you're going to Thailand. What if a big neon sign flashed in your mind that said: *Stop, no more new countries, you've exceeded your limit, your brain will not be able to hold any new images of elephants or appreciate traditional Thai costumes and dances or appreciate the exotic flavors of Thai food. You've already been to six foreign countries. That's your limit.* There is no limit. I once sat on the plane next to an executive from the Coca-Cola Company. His job was to open up new markets in countries around the world. I asked him how many he had visited and he said he had been to 160 countries. Wow! He would have been way past his limit. There is no limit to human potential. Grow, baby, grow.

The Racecourse of Life

In the previous section of the book, we discussed your desire, your passion, and your determination to do what you *want* with your life. To summarize a few key points, if you are principled-centered and know what you want and have a vision of where you're going, you are really ready to zoom on the racecourse of life. So what is left in order to get your music out, achieve your goals, and do your dreams? The answer: the *Investment* and the *Commitment* to stay the course. To use the race analogy one more time, you may have learned the principles of successful racing, you may want to do your best to win the race, and you may have a vision of yourself crossing the finish line ahead of other cars. This is great. You are ready. However, you will still need to buy a car and hire a crew to maintain it. Plus, you will need to learn how to operate the car and do your daily laps to stay in practice. Finally, you will need to demonstrate fortitude and endurance as you join the race.

Do the Work...Love the Work!

Let me offer a slightly different analogy that is meaningful to me. I love to ride my bicycle. It is about the man-mind-machine connection, the outdoors, and great exercise. When we talk about *Vision*, we think of ourselves looking upward to the horizon ahead. I have made an interesting discovery about riding my bicycle up mountains. There is a time to look up at the top of the hill to see where I intend to go and then there is a time to put my head down, look at the road just in front of me, crank the pedals, and do the work. I must do this for the required amount of time for the required distance to achieve my goals and to realize the vision I initially had. There is no way around it. However, once I get in the rhythm of doing the work, I begin to enjoy the journey and become even more determined to stay the course. I focus on the work. When I sense that I have done sufficient work, I lift my head up slightly and delight in the revelation that I'm almost there. I've done it! Had I instead become engaged in wishful thinking by dwelling on the exciting vision too long, I might have grown weary because the goal would seem "far off" for a long time. As I concentrate on a short piece of road just ahead of me, each little stretch goes by fast and my sense of progress is enhanced. Life by the yard is hard. Life by the inch is a cinch. This is the message about doing the work required to achieve your goals.

We often hear "no pain, no gain." There is a friendlier way to express this principle. To get what you want, you've got to figure out what you need to give as your investment in success and as your commitment to doing your part. I remember reading an interview with Michael Jordan. The interviewer remarked that to be as good as Michael was/is at the game of basketball, he must have had to give 110 percent to the game and to his practice on the court and in the gym. Michael responded that it was absolutely not about giving 110 percent but about giving whatever it takes and the whole thing is about how much you want whatever "it" happens to be. How much you want "it" determines how much you're willing to give.

Do You Really, Really Want to Succeed?

Do you want to be successful? Why? Is it a really big, important, glorious, exciting reason? It needs to be so, for only with powerful desire and motivation—the "why-to"—will you be prepared to make the investment and show the commitment to your goals that will make it all possible. Once you've got the "why-to" in place, then you can worry about the "how-to." At this point, you will then be determined to find the resources you need, learn the skills you need, and do the work that is required. You will get from life great things as you give your very best to life.

The stories to support this Leverage Key are so numerous. Every heroic sports story we've ever witnessed, heard, or watched on TV or at the movies is a testimonial to this principle of giving of yourself to get what you want. Let me share a story that's not from the sports pages.

To Truly Understand

I once read about a famous doctor who had always admired Mother Teresa, as I do. Mother Teresa was planning a trip to Mexico City to minister to the poor. The good doctor approached her and asked if he could join her entourage to witness her work firsthand, to photograph her among the people of Mexico City, and to better understand her ministry. She responded to this effect, "My good friend, I am honored that you wish to accompany me. You are welcome to do so. However, to better understand my ministry, I would invite you to take the money you would spend on airfare and lodging, to sell your camera, and then give these monies to the poor. Then you will truly understand my ministry."

Sometimes in life, we want to "get the experience" and derive the benefits without making the investment. We may listen to a patriotic song and feel emotionally choked up about our great nation and then fail to vote on Election Day. That's not how a true spirit of patriotism comes about. We may hope to win the lottery as the easy road to financial security. This is not how it's going to happen. If it is to be, it is up to you to give, to learn, to overcome the obstacles, to find the resources, to pay the price, and to take the steps necessary to win the prize in the race of life. Now that you know what you want, what must you now prepare yourself to give? Return to the list of 16 wants in the previous chapter and contemplate what it would take to do each dream and turn your wants to reality. It's worth it.

Leverage Key 10

The Best Investment You'll Ever Make

In his new-millennium book, *The Circle of Innovation*, Tom Peters, speaking of the power of the Internet said, "The computer is not the point, even if it is a matchless/revolutionary enabling device. The point: *human relationships*. Okay?"

That's quite a statement for the pure techies out there. But even the most technologically proficient individuals would have to agree that it's not just that the Internet gives us a new tool to help manage the information age. The Internet gives us a whole new way of forming and sustaining relationships around the globe, from your den or the back corner of your bedroom or from your laptop, wherever it is.

Our company Website has proven to be a fascinating presence on the world stage. Not only do we find new business prospects, but we also make some interesting friends along the way (who could become prospects one day). A few months ago, I received an e-mail from a Chinese student in Singapore who had just visited our Website. He said, "Mr. Checketts, I notice that you do Customer Service training. I am writing a paper for my business class on the importance of customer care. Would you recommend some books for me to study as I prepare?" How cool, I got to help a student many thousands of miles away with his term paper and recommend my own books and others. It didn't take long. And I'm a firm believer that what goes around comes around. One day, I'll bump into this "student" after he has become Director of Customer Service for Singapore Global Industries. He'll remember. What a human connector the Internet is. It has totally changed our relationships with customers. These relationships have evolved from periodic phone calls to minute-by-minute, real-time interactions.

The Internet brings a whole new dimension to parenthood and grandparenthood. Some of our off-spring live many miles away and yet we get weekly and sometimes daily news bulletins on their comings and goings, their challenges and accomplishments.

It's All About Relationships

Well, if the Internet is about relationships, isn't everything? Why do we do anything? What is the impact of anything you do? Don't we do things to change relationships, at some level? The most significant consequences of the things we do impact our relation-ships in some way. Unless you're a hermit or operate a forest service lookout tower, the biggest cause and effect outcomes of life are about relationships. And even the lookout tower operator is helping to manage the relationships between nature and nearby communities and those who visit the forest. When you buy a house and move in, you change the relationships among those who already live in the neighborhood. When you get your financing through a local bank, you form a relationship with the mortgage officer. If you choose a local bank, you affect the relationship between your local community and the national economy. The balance of funds may shift closer to home rather than to a larger institution across the country somewhere. When you pull your car onto the freeway, you change the relationship of all the other drivers. Some must back off. Some must go around you. Some may be angry with you. You form an attitude about these other drivers who "share" the road with you.

The Force...The Multiplier Effect

We are all so interconnected that to ignore relationships would be to ignore the most important investment opportunity of all. Vision is *The Force*. Strong desire is leverage. However, all of these powers we have discussed, on their own, are personal power factors. The minute you involve others in your vision, the minute your desires impact others, all of your personal power factors will benefit from the multiplier effect. This is real leverage. It is obvious that, when you alone hold a vision, you speak with one small voice. When you recruit others to the cause, you speak with a high-fidelity, mega-watt sound system. When a client comes to me and says, "What we have to do is nearly impossible," my suggestion is, "nothing is impossible with the right partnerships." Partnerships are relationships with a powerful purpose to make things happen. If you must do the impossible, get more partners. Build the relationships.

Blessed Are the Flexible

Relationships are about *flexibility, respect, communication,* and *trust.* The ultimate indication that a relationship is working well is the existence of *trust.* You can hear trust. You can see trust. You can feel it in the air. When I work with teams, I pick up on break-room gossip. I see the CYA (Cover Your Anatomy) e-mails. Some conversation is loaded with office politics. Where various trust gaps exist, the root causes are generally communication gaps. And with whom do we communicate faithfully and openly? With those we *respect.* If you don't respect someone, you forget to invite him or her to the meeting. You probably don't stop by their desk to chat or send them an FYI copy of some important bulletin. What is more serious, you really don't take the time to listen to their ideas. You'd just as soon avoid any interaction in the first place.

Communication is the way we manifest respect and build trust. Even more fundamentally, good relationships begin with *flexibility.* A great reminder is: *Oh, blessed are the flexible, for they shall not get bent out of shape.* Only by being flexible are we willing to give "strangers" the benefit of the doubt and communicate at all. As we do, we often find new friends in "strange" places. Then, respect, inside new relationships, has a chance to flourish. To quote Frank A. Clark, "We find comfort among those who agree with us—growth among those who don't."

"Dad, How Come You Work with Idiots?"

I'll never forget the man in one of my seminars who raised his hand and goodheartedly shared this: "Darby, the other night when I came home from work, my young son asked me, 'Dad, how come you work with idiots?' I realized that the night before I had been sharing my work frustrations with my wife and my son had overhead me tell her 'what a bunch of idiots I worked with.' Of course, I was just using the word 'idiots' loosely, probably too loosely." As I recently worked with one new client group, they came to an agreement that to change the spirit of their team and their approach to customers, they would need to drop the phrase "stupid customers" from their conversations. What a symbolic realization this was for the group.

So, how do you invest in relationships?

Give Time. There's no substitute for spending time with others whose alliance you need and who depend on you.

Show Flexibility. One of my most important principles of professional conduct is this: *Reserve Judgment.* While first impressions are crucial, they are so often inaccurate. It takes discipline to create good first impressions and even greater discipline to get past the first impressions we form of others.

Gain Knowledge. You can't possibly know too much about the backgrounds, circumstances, wants, and needs of those in your circle of family, friends, and influence. Walk a mile in their shoes. At least go to a couple of their meetings if it's a business relationship that's involved. I am always amazed at how often someone will say, "If our customers would just give us more

notice and let us know what they're planning to do...."
I respond, "Can you go to their quarterly planning
meetings?" I get that "I just discovered the Grand Canyon"
look.

Communicate, Communicate. Communication is
for two primary purposes: (a) to understand and be
sure you're understood, and (b) to learn where you
stand with others and help them know where they stand
with you. The first of these purposes is about
information...ideas, opinions, concerns, and so on. The
second of these is all about *relationships*. Often, what
is not said or the nonverbal communication is more
important that the actual words exchanged. There are
the words we say and the impressions we convey. The
words are usually about "stuff," the *impressions* are
usually about "us" and signal to others whether respect
is present or not and whether trust is growing or not.
For example: "Son, I'm surprised you have so much
trouble with your math homework. It's pretty basic."
Those last three words (among others) actually send the
message: "You're either not smart enough or you're
lazy." By contrast, consider: "Son, that math homework must be trickier than I realize. Is there anything
I can do to help?"

Relationship Investment Guides

There are many "investment guides" on effective
communication and relationship building. I invite you
to read two of my other books: *Customer Astonishment:
10 Secrets to World-Class Customer Care* and *Dancing in
Peanut Butter*. Be certain to read these three extremely
relevant books by my great friend and business partner,
Steve Chandler: *Relationshift, 50 Ways to Create Great
Relationships,* and *100 Ways to Motivate Others*. One of my

all-time favorite books on the subject of communication is the all-so-practical and timeless classic, *Getting to Yes,* by Roger Fisher and William Ury.

Be a Connector

In his best-selling book, *The Tipping Point*, Malcolm Gladwell describes those among us who are *Connectors*. These individuals have a remarkable gift for initiating and perpetuating relationships. Mr. Gladwell gives the example of Paul Revere. Here is an excerpt. Please don't be intimidated by Paul Revere's example. Admire it. Be thankful for it. And commit to connecting people and to building the relationships that make anything possible. Paul Revere changed our world. He helped to build a nation based on powerful and purposeful relationships.

> *Here, then, is the explanation for why Paul Revere's midnight ride started a word-of-mouth epidemic...He was a Connector. He was, for example, gregarious and intensely social. When he died, his funeral was attended, in the words of one contemporary newspaper account, by "troops of people." He was a fisherman and a hunter, a cardplayer and theater-lover, a frequenter of pubs and a successful businessman. He was active in the local Masonic Lodge and was a member of several select social clubs. He was also a doer, a man blessed—as David Hackett Fischer recounts— with an "uncanny genius for being the center of events"....It is not surprising, then, that when the British army began its secret campaign in 1774 to root out and destroy the stores of arms and ammunition held by the fledgling revolutionary movement, Revere became a kind of unofficial clearing house*

for the anti-British forces. He knew everybody. He was the logical one to go to if you were a stable boy on the afternoon of April 18th, 1775, and overheard two British officers talking about how there would be hell to pay on the following afternoon. Nor is it surprising that when Revere set out for Lexington that night, he would have known just how to spread the news as far and wide as possible. When he saw people on the roads, he was so naturally and irrepressibly social he would have stopped and told them. When he came upon a town, he would have known exactly whose door to knock on, who the local militia leader was, and who the key players in town were. He had met most of them before. And they knew and respected him as well.

What an investment in relationships Paul Revere made. What a return on that investment we have all experienced.

Leverage Key 11

The Big Picture: Combining Direction With Perspective

Just how B-I-G can you think? One of the truly great companies out there is DuPont. A close friend of mine did extensive consulting with them at a time when their commitment to renewed excellence could be summed up by a question that was their standard of performance and creativity: *What is theoretically possible?* It is interesting that a "standard" would occur in the form of a question. When an individual or a team at DuPont would undertake some new project and set their performance goals—whether for cost reduction, quality, market penetration, and so on—the question would be raised, "And what is theoretically possible?" We'll call this the WITP question.

What Is Theoretically Possible?

I enjoy this WITP exercise with my client training groups. I ask what is theoretically possible in terms of the size of a cell phone. Responses are typically, "the size of a credit card" or "how about a wristwatch?" We soon realize that these quantum leaps are aggressive, but not the answer. When folks think about a credit card or a wristwatch, they're still thinking they need a place for a small keypad and a tiny lithium battery. What is theoretically possible is on the order of a microdot glued to the side of your rear molar. How is it powered? The movement of your jaw powers it. How do you dial up? You softly speak your password and the name of the person or place you wish to call. How do you hear it without an earpiece? The sound is a small vibration against your tooth that is transmitted via your jawbone directly into your inner ear. This is super high-fidelity sound transmission, in fact. How do you hang up the phone? You gently click your teeth together. How much does it cost? It's free. What if the glue comes loose and you swallow it? It's really not a problem with a microdot. Are telecommunication companies working on such a product? Of course they are.

We are in an age when we must set what I call C-BIG goals. C stands for three C-words: *Crazy*, *Courageous*, and *Creative*. We must be all three. Crazy is a great word because it is the test as to whether you are really thinking big enough. When someone says, "That goal's crazy. It's impossible," and they chuckle, you know you're on the right track. If you don't See-BIG, you won't see enough. Once we have purpose, vision, and goals, we have *direction*, but there is a balancing factor still needed. It is *Perspective*. Having a sense of direction means you know *where* you're going. Having perspective means you know the environment through which you're going. For example, imagine that you plotted a course from point A in central Florida to point B and laid out a nice straight course to get there. Your course looks good on paper. However, depending on the quality of the map you used, you may not be aware of all the waterways and swamps that lie in your path. You would probably need to take a drive, or better yet, a helicopter ride to see all that you might encounter along your way, including alligators.

Take a Helicopter Ride

In order to set C-BIG goals, you will always benefit from a helicopter ride, actual or virtual, to gain perspective. Let's take one now. Get ready. Just outside the front door, our helicopter is waiting. Go ahead. Walk over to the helicopter. Those big whirring blades are about nine feet in the air above us. Don't worry, you won't get an unexpected haircut on your way to the door. Jump in. Close the door. Fasten your seat belt. Put on your earphones and away we go. Up. Up. Up. The sound of the rotors is "whap, whap, whap." We're twisting in the wind a little. It's quite exciting. Dipping to the right and then to the left. Wow!

What a view. What do you see? The cars look like little insects scurrying along those pathways we call highways. Suddenly the stuff that seemed so big and important on the ground is now small and just blends into one great panorama of neighborhoods, blending into a city, blending into a society and into a vast geography and, yes, even a vast economic system of things. What can you see from up here in the helicopter that you couldn't see down on the ground?

Wow! Do you realize how much money someone has made simply producing rearview mirrors for all those cars down there? What if you had a contract to supply just the replacement light bulbs for the street lights you see lined up down there? By the way, does it matter right now that Joe, the guy whose desk is next to yours, is sort of a cranky fellow and that no one bothered to fill up the paper tray on your office copier this morning? Nope. What matters right now is the world going 'round. Can you and your team of work associates, or you and the neighbors in your community, have any impact on what is going on in this big picture you now see?

Up ahead is the industrial park where your company offices are located. Do you know who works in those seven other buildings in the park? Are any of these companies selling to the same customers your company sells to? What does it mean for your business that a new shopping mall is going up just over there, to the right, in that large tract of land that has been vacant for so long? There's the university campus and a large group of state government buildings. Did you ever wonder why your company tends to focus its marketing efforts on other private sector companies? Why has no one approached government agencies and the university?

Where does most of the material your company uses in making its products come from? Los Angeles? What if the interstate highway system leading to you from the west was shut down by a natural disaster for a number of weeks? What would this do to your business?

Does your company have an alternative source of supply from the east? Yikes!

Another helicopter just whizzed by. It's the Channel 5 news helicopter. How come your company never gets in the news? Is yours "just one more company"? Does the community even know the cool stuff you do? Are you considered leaders in your industry and in the community?

It's time to land. That was fun. Your mind was racing at a new pace, at new levels of thinking. Oh well, back to work. No, it's back to business. Business is exciting. You wonder what you can do to revolutionize your company's business opportunities. For starters, it's time to find out who else shares your industrial park. It's time to ask the marketing department why they don't do business with government agencies and the university.

And what's the latest breakthrough your company has created that deserves some community recognition? Do you and other people out there appreciate what you all manage to do down here on solid ground or is it somehow lost in the hustle and bustle and the noise here at street level? It's time to examine your goals. Here's where to begin, with the 21st Century Standard of Performance Excellence: What is theoretically possible?

Consider these applications of the great WITP question.

- ✓ How fast are we at turning around customer orders? *What is theoretically possible?*
- ✓ How cost-effective is our work process? *What is theoretically possible?*
- ✓ How reliable are our products? *What is theoretically possible?*

- ✓ How much leverage do we get from computer technology? *What is theoretically possible?*
- ✓ How well-coordinated are the efforts of our work team? *What is theoretically possible?*
- ✓ How quick are we to express appreciation for quality work and dependability? *What is theoretically possible?*
- ✓ How creative are we? *What is theoretically possible?*

Now, shift from work to home...

- ✓ How do we encourage learning in our home, as a family? *What is theoretically possible?*
- ✓ How much fun do we have together? *What is theoretically possible?*
- ✓ How well do we listen to each other? *What is theoretically possible?*
- ✓ How much are we saving for vacations, home improvements, and our retirement? *What is theoretically possible?*
- ✓ How many miles per gallon does our family car get? *What is theoretically possible?*

The WITP question is a fun eye-opener and an invitation to See-BIG, so that you do see the big world that wraps around your goals and your plans. Once you see the bigger picture, you can also put things in perspective.

The Bigger Picture...
The Inner Vision

There is one other important dimension to your ever-broadening perspective. It goes beyond seeing the big picture with your physical eyes. It is about seeing the world with a special set of eyes, with a sort of x-ray vision that let's you see inside yourself to understand why some things matter more than others and where your priorities should be set. These eyes have an "optical" nerve that connects back to your other sense of vision, to your sense of purpose, to the voice of the cricket, and to the principles that center you. These eyes let you see the potential of your 13-year-old son. These eyes let you see the need for a neighborhood barbecue. These eyes let you see a fellow employee who needs recognition. These eyes let you see the big sign on the freeway of life that says, "Slow down, take in the scenery, and enjoy the moment."

Take a helicopter ride now and then. See what you don't see on the ground. Or see what is important that's right under your nose and is otherwise blocked

Leverage Key 12

Ownership and Stewardship

I call my great author friend and coach Steve Chandler, "The Voice of Ownership." He is also the world's leading expert on channel changers. By channel changers, I refer to the remote control devices we use to operate our TVs and the special channel changers we use to operate our lives. Some individuals choose to really OWN their channel changers. There are those who let others take control of their channel changers and PUSH their buttons. This leads to considerable frustration and a sense of powerlessness. This cycle happens in the family room when you argue over what to watch on TV, and it happens in life when you lose the spirit of ownership and let yourself become a victim of your circumstances.

The Greatest Secret of the Ages

At the heart of understanding the channel changer of life is the discovery, or rediscovery, of the greatest secret of the ages: *You create your world by how you think and speak about it.* There is never just one world outside your window. There's whatever world you think it is. One person sees rain clouds and says, "Oh no, it's going to rain. Our picnic plans will be ruined." Another person sees rain clouds and says, "Hooray, it's going to rain. Our garden will be saved." The person thinking about picnics sees one world. The person thinking about gardens sees another. And all the thinking or speaking about rain isn't going to change anything about the rain. The thinking and speaking will only change your world. And here's the amazing thing about life, you can change your thoughts and change your world as quickly and as easily as you can push different buttons on your TV's remote control.

Two Systems: Owner and Victim

There are two powerful channels or systems that we access with our mental channel changers: the *Owner* system and the *Victim* system. The person accessing the *Owner* system takes responsibility for situations and outcomes. The person accessing the *Victim* system simply figures that "stuff happens and you must struggle through it somehow."

To further contrast these systems, consider the "owner" person who is busy getting from life all that she or he can in terms of learning, strength, experience, excitement, and more. Conversely, the "victim" person is focused on just getting through the week to have some "free time" on the weekend, "getting through those teenage years with our kids," or just getting through to retirement. The happiness of life is always "out there" somewhere hopefully waiting for the beleaguered person to get through whatever's getting in the way at the moment. And it is the moment at hand that holds the only real promise for happiness there is. The "owner" will seize that moment and create the world around it.

Perhaps the most powerful owner-victim contrast is about commitment. Once upon a time, the saddest phrase of tongue or pen was, "It might have been." Today, I think the saddest phrase of tongue (or pen) is, "I'm sort of committed." It is technically impossible to be "sort of committed." In the Victim system, commitment is just a feeling. In the Owner system, commitment is a decision. What does it mean when someone says, "You know, our company is just not the same company it was five or 10 years ago. I'm not feeling as committed as I used to." That's the language of "feeling" discouraged, disconnected, and NOT committed. The owner mentality goes like this, "The business has changed, but as long as I choose to butter my bread here, this must be the best darned company in town."

Consider this about where you work. If you "feel" it is a dumb place to work, why would you work there much longer? Okay, if it's the only job you could possibly qualify for in the entire free world, I understand. Or if you are three hours and 27 minutes away from cashing in on a fantastic retirement program, I understand. Otherwise, I would question why a smart person would work for a dumb company when there are plenty of smart companies out there. You are either committed to your

work or not. What you feel about your work is something else. The owner grabs the channel changer and
begins to deal with whatever the obstacles may be—
to remove these or navigate around them. The owner
loves what is. The owner wastes no time in self-pity.

I want to finish this chapter with one of the greatest
examples of ownership and stewardship I know. Aha,
new concept: "stewardship." You see, once someone
discovers the ownership spirit, that individual accepts
responsibility for the work, the problems, the relationships, the opportunities, and all that life has sent
in his or her direction. *Ownership* on the inside leads
naturally to *stewardship* on the outside.

The Continuing Saga
of Peter Madike

Do you remember Peter Madike of Ikeja? Return
with me to Nigeria. For a moment, imagine how easy
it would be to feel discouraged, even angry about your
circumstances, living in a developing country and
finding yourself among those who are impoverished
and underprivileged, by the world's standards.

During my second trip to Nigeria and after having spent several weeks with Peter Madike, I began to
reflect on how much effort Peter had to expend to
earn $60 per month to provide for a family of eight.
And as I came to so fully appreciate his helpfulness
and protection, I felt I needed to provide some sort
of special reward to him that would help his financial
situation. At the end of my visit, I chose to give him
$300. This was the equivalent of five months pay. I
was somewhat afraid this could spoil him and make
him discontent with his wage. As much as I trusted

Peter, I realized that it would be a natural inclination for many people (including myself) to take such a windfall and splurge. Conversely, my hope was that this would be a substantial financial breakthrough for Peter and his dear family. I chose to bet on his wisdom.

Peter was emotionally overwhelmed when I handed him the money. He could not speak. He did not believe his eyes. I gave him a hug as tears filled my eyes.

The Test and the Triumph

When I returned to Nigeria a year later, I was curious to learn how Peter had spent the $300. I realized that if it had slipped away he would be embarrassed to tell me, so I chose to not bring up the subject. It was not long after my arrival that Peter announced that he was excited to take me back to his home to show me what he had done with the money I had given him many months ago. With a slight apologetic tone in his voice, he admitted that he had spent a few dollars on pineapple for a family celebration the day I gave him the money. He also purchased some used shoes for his children. "But," he said, "You must come to my home to see what I bought with most of the money." We jumped in the car and headed for Ikeja.

When we arrived at Peter's home, Adankwo stood in the doorway beaming about something. I thought she was glad to see me. She was, but she was mostly beaming with pride. We walked into the main room of their apartment and there in the middle of the floor was a strange wooden machine. The machine was handmade. It had a large lever that opened and closed two wooden members in a clamp-like fashion. There was an electric cord running from the electrical outlet and up the side of the machine to connect with copper wires inside the jaws of the wooden clamp. A large roll of thin plastic sheeting hung from the opposite side of the wooden frame and was draped across the machine, then threaded through the clamp-like mechanism. Peter explained that the machine was for making plastic bags. The copper wires inside the jaws of the clamp would become hot. The plastic sheeting could be folded from side to side inside the clamp. When the lever closed the clamp, the two copper wires on the top and the bottom of clamp would melt and fuse the edges of the plastic together. Sections of the folded sheeting would be cut and then fused along the other open edge to form a plastic bag. Finished bags would be put in bundles to sell to shoppers at the food bazaar for use in collecting beans, grain, fruit, vegetables, and other foods sold only in bulk.

Adankwo, Homemaker and Businesswoman

Peter had invested in a plastic bag-making machine so that Adankwo could operate a simple business from her home while the children played nearby. Peter was not a victim of his circumstances. He was an entrepreneur and investor. He used most of the $300 to leverage his family's income. And to think, he had never attended the *Ownership Spirit* seminar. While so many benefit from the instruction Steve Chandler and I give, there are those who are so naturally principle-centered. They teach us by their example. Peter had somehow internalized the principles of frugality and of investing in the future. My $300 gift had been used to create an additional income stream for the Madike family. What could possibly be better?

Peter Madike, Owner!

Peter is an owner. He loves what is. He is a steward. He takes responsibility for what life gives. If it gives him joy, he celebrates. If it gives him challenges, he creates. There are those who wait for better circumstances and those who create the circumstances they need to succeed. Grab your channel changer. Push the button that says "owner," and turn up the volume.

Leverage Key 13

Leadership and Influence

I checked in at the registration table, took my seminar packet, and went inside the auditorium to enjoy another opportunity to learn about a favorite subject: leadership. The instructor took the microphone and said, "Good morning. I am here to give you the shortest, most to-the-point leadership seminar you've ever experienced. Are you ready? Please take notes. The three most important elements of effective leadership are: example, example, example. (Pause) Thank you."

And then the instructor sat down. He sat there for about two minutes while the audience puzzled, pondered, and then began to whisper, "He's right, but do you think the seminar's really over?"

Well, you can imagine the outcome. The instructor returned to the front of the platform and went on to share many other interesting concepts about leadership.

But he was right, I believe. The greatest of leaders not only walk the talk, they *live* the talk. And some can live the message without even the need to talk. When we are around them, we know what's important. We know what they expect of us, because it's what they expect of themselves. We can follow them on the bedrock basis of *trust*.

Your Heroes

I invite you to do this simple exercise. Write down the names of two or three of your special heroes who are also effective leaders...people you would follow on a basis of trust. For each of the heroes on your list, identify several characteristics (qualities or virtues) you admire about these leaders. Once you have done this, you will have at least three insights.

1. What you have just done is a very simple, uncomplicated "values identification" exercise. The leadership qualities you wrote down are closely akin to your own "core values" in life.

2. These characteristics also suggest the behaviors you would expect great leaders to cultivate and demonstrate.

3. At the same time, these qualities are likely to be those you already represent to others, as you consciously or subconsciously follow the examples of the leaders you admire. What a positive, reassuring, and perhaps surprising insight this is.

You, the Hero

We all know we are often our own worst critics. We look out there at others who we see as successful and say to ourselves, "I wish I could be like him or her." Perhaps you already are. Give yourself credit. If you did not already operate on the basis of positive values and if you were not already striving to become a better version of who you are, you probably wouldn't be reading this book. You are already on the right track. By reaching out, by looking forward, and by committing yourself to personal growth, you are leading. You may be the very leader your family, friends, and work associates look to for guidance and support. They admire your example. You know and they know you're not perfect, but what's wrong with that? People want to be led by real people, authentic people, and not necessarily perfect people. It's time to give yourself a little pat on the back and say, "I am becoming a good leader. One of my prime commitments is to keep growing. This is why I am reading this book on 'lifting my world' and gaining the further leverage I need to make a difference."

True Humility

It is good that, along with your leadership qualities, you possess sufficient humility that you retain your openness to the ideas of others. You cultivate a willingness to learn and to grow and to acknowledge those who share their ideas and support you.

My father taught me a great lesson about true humility. He said, "Son, humility is often misunderstood as being self-deprecating. What that means, son, is some people feel they must belittle themselves or be apologetic to be humble. Instead, true humility is giving credit exactly where credit is due and sometimes to honestly give yourself some of the credit."

He went on to explain that if someone complimented me on the beautiful brown color of my eyes, I should not take any credit and be very humble. I would need to give credit to God and to "good genes" for my eyes. If I came up with a creative solution to some problem based on suggestions from others, true humility would be to surely give credit to the sources of my knowledge and insight. If in presenting this solution, I worked long and hard into the midnight hours to create a great speech and someone came up after the speech to congratulate me, I should say, "Thank you very much. I worked very hard on that speech and I am so pleased that it was helpful to you." True humility is giving credit exactly where credit is due.

As I shared previously, my greatest leader heroes are Gandhi, Henry V, and Lawrence of Arabia. Gandhi's oft-quoted admonition, "You must be the change you hope to see in others," is the ultimate challenge to exemplary leadership. It is notable that Gandhi always retained his humility. He knew the responsibility he had to use his growing power and influence wisely. He had earned the respect of millions and was deeply humbled by this realization and by the magnitude of his calling.

It's important that we not miss the leverage in humility and that we see that there's no contradiction when a leader possesses both power and humility. In life, we often encounter two seeming opposites that must somehow coexist. These subtle leverage points are sometimes called "dichotomies." Great leaders, such as Gandhi, become "Masters of Dichotomies." We will see how.

By stark contrast to Gandhi, Lawrence of Arabia seemed to lose his humility in the end as he became self-possessed of his own passions. The once noble cause he pursued became too much the cause of Lawrence of Arabia, the individual, rather than the cause of those he served. In the process, "the cause" lost much of its nobility and a great leader lost his leverage.

A Leader's Leader

Henry V demonstrated his balanced capacity for leadership by discerning how to motivate his followers in the face of frightening opposition and the prospect of death. His ability to inspire was demonstrated in the famous speech he delivered on St. Crispin's Day. This ability was not the result of mere eloquence. It grew out of his genuine commitment and love for his men as demonstrated so subtly and so profoundly the night before the great speech. Let me retell the story briefly:

As King Henry prepared to lead his men to battle with a French army 20 times the size of his own, he knew he had to lift these weary (yet still courageous) warriors to perform heroic deeds. His lieutenants alerted him to the fact that there were considerable murmurings among the men and that they were beginning to have serious doubts about their ability to survive the coming battles. And as much as they loved King Henry, they were even beginning to doubt his wisdom in choosing to confront the French. Henry knew he must deliver a mighty speech before their fateful encounter. The night before the battle, he saw his men huddled around their campfires. Their bodies were stooped with shoulders rounded. Their countenances were ashen.

King Henry knew his task would require more strength than he alone possessed. He went into the shadows of the woods to turn his thoughts heavenward and plead for godly power to fortify himself and to be able to reach into the souls of his men. After his supplications, he returned to the campfires. On the way, he put on an everyman's cloak to disguise himself, so that he could mingle with his men, unrecognized as their king. He needed to hear their thoughts and understand their beliefs about the task that lie before them. As he moved from one campfire to another, he sat quietly and listened to what they feared would happen on the battleground, his plans became clear. On the basis of what he learned, he formulated every word he would speak to prepare them for the battle he was determined to win with them at his side.

When the morning came, young King Henry turned the tide of belief and the tide of human events by one of the greatest speeches ever given by a leader. The speech gave credit exactly where credit would be due, to his men and their valor, which he let them know he knew they still possessed. His belief in them saved the day. They would later honor him for his inspiration and his example as he led them into the heat of battle. And yet, at every turn King Henry demonstrated his undying loyalty to his men. Together, they ruled the day.

Be a Master of Dichotomies

Great leaders master dichotomies. As you operate your business, there will be many opportunities to do this. You will hear admonitions that seem contradictory, such as: "You must run a tight ship" versus "We have to be flexible." The question will arise, "How will you do both? The leader will answer, "Yes. Yes we will do both. We will be firm about WHAT our goals and commitments are. At the same time, we will be flexible and creative as to HOW we approach the fulfillment of these goals and meet our commitments." Thus, you begin to see *the power of opposites*.

The Power of Opposites

On one hand, "You must leave nothing to chance." On the other hand, "You must delegate and trust others." The answer: We will leave nothing to chance by trusting each other. This means, we will need to have clear agreements and be skillful so that trusting in each other leaves little or nothing to chance.

On the one hand, "Failure is not an option." On the other hand, "To fail is to learn." The answer: To fail at the outset as we try new things is to learn. To make the same mistake repeatedly is not an option.

On one hand, "You must be decisive." On the other hand, "You must listen to the counsel of others." The answer: A leader will be teachable and open to the counsel of others and yet decisive and courageous enough to gratefully acknowledge and reject that counsel from time to time.

On one hand, "A leader needs to be powerful and influential." On the other hand, "A leader needs to be humble." The answer: *You must be the change you hope to see in others.*

The Greatest Leverage of All

Finally, a leader does need the *Leverage* available in these dichotomies. Leverage is extending your power through others to accomplish something far greater than your own agenda. "Give me a lever long enough and a place to stand, and I could lift the world," said Archimedes. Knowing what is in the hearts of your followers is leverage. It gives you the ability to inspire them for *what wins the heart will rule the mind.* Genuine humility is leverage. It becomes the basis for earning the trust of others. This trust is the greatest leverage of all.

Leverage Key 14

Truth

We have discussed the idea of being principle-centered. The value of such a commitment to principles is in direct proportion to the soundness of the principles we choose. As we choose, it is the truth we seek. This truth gives us especially solid footing in our quest for leverage to lift the world. How do we define truth? Let us consider three bases for defining truth and the combination of these: (1) God, (2) Science, (3) What Works. There is a fourth basis for defining truth and that is with some sort of relativity to times, places, persons, and a somewhat arbitrary assignment of "truth." The trouble with this relativity is that principles based on these "truths" would not stand the test of time (meaning the test of a lot of time). The truest principles would stand the test of time and prove reliable anywhere, anytime, with anybody who wished to apply them.

The Golden Rule

I was teaching a seminar in Philadelphia. The subject was "team effectiveness" and how to improve working relationships. As the conversation progressed, I asked the audience for examples of guiding principles. One older man raised his hand and said, "The Golden Rule." A fellow next to him laughed and said, "Oh yeah, them that has the gold rule." I managed to acknowledge the first contributor and still chuckle at the other man's editorial on The Golden Rule. Other people joined in and remarked that The Golden Rule was a tried and proven concept most of us had learned from our grandparents.

Then, one young woman stood up with just an ounce of indignation and chided me. She said, "I beg your pardon, Mr. Checketts, but aren't you plagiarizing just a little? You should be giving credit to the person who has cultivated and taught this concept of 'do unto others.' It's in his book. Wasn't it Stephen Covey?" She was serious. The audience went silent. Then some folks started to chuckle. I managed to reply with a straight face, "Thank you for your comment. I do acknowledge Stephen Covey who has taught us many great things. I have read his books. I know him personally. Quite frankly, this concept of 'Do unto others as you would have them do unto you' dates back considerably before Mr. Covey. In fact, it goes back about 2,000 years." I then saw her tablemate give her the elbow and say, "It was Jesus Christ, not Stephen Covey."

I choose to accept that there is a grand confluence of truth that we can trust without a debate over science versus religion. I choose to look for core truths that are reliable and likely to play some very clear and lasting role in the operation of the universe and the betterment of humankind.

I believe God is not arbitrary. God operates on the basis of timeless laws and true principles. Science would acknowledge that timeless laws and true principles would have to be in operation to have any hope of rationalizing the stupendous creation that is our universe. Thus, there is a huge and reliable body of truth for us to discover. Where is it? Who possesses it? How do we find it? I like to think of the quest for truth this way....

The Wondrous Intergalactic Puzzle

Once upon a time, in a galaxy far away, God gathered us all together to explain that we would each have the opportunity to take on a physical form and live here on earth. God explained that the quality of the experience would be determined by how much we learned and by how well we treated each other. We would not be given a set of step-by-step instructions. We would each search for the truth. Some would discover more truths than others. Those with large portions of truth would be our teachers. Our quest for truth would be similar to assembling a puzzle. Certain pieces of the puzzle we would craft for ourselves based on our own learning. Our teachers would give us other important puzzle pieces. Some teachers would have an especially "big picture" and help us complete large sections of the puzzle at once. Perhaps we would share pieces of the puzzle with each other. Whether we physically possessed the pieces or not, we would increasingly have the picture we were seeking revealed to our view. The pieces of the puzzle would be scattered across the earth and found in every land and be nurtured by a diversity of spiritual traditions, by a variety of intellectual pursuits, and by many scientific endeavors. Some pieces of the puzzle would be best discernible through logic. Other pieces would require an intuitive or instinctive appreciation. It would be required that *faith* accompanies *knowledge* to fully comprehend the puzzle picture and its message.

In this quest for truth, it would be a liability to narrow the search too soon—to possibly exclude pieces of the truth puzzle waiting to be found in faraway or unfamiliar places. As we would happen upon the truth puzzle pieces, we would rejoice and choose to anchor ourselves in these truths. More and more, we would be inclined to share these truths with others. As we gained more truth, and with it wisdom, a sense of inclusiveness would help move us away from prejudice, hatred, and war that would otherwise result when those with certain clusters of truth competed for credibility and proclaimed sole command of the truth. We would accept the idea that truth cannot be imposed on others, that each of us must discover the truth for ourselves to find the surest footing for life's adventure. And the greatest truth discoveries of all would be to discover who we are and what we mean to each other. As we did, the probability would be high that we would choose *The Golden Rule*.

Leverage Key 15

Force Fields

We may have experienced the end of the official Star Wars age. George Lucas indicated that Episode III would be the last. On the other hand, while the series of motion pictures may be complete, we will hope that *The Force* is with us for many years to come.

Earth: The Brightest Star?

There are many forces at work around us, within us, and upon us. I recall this intriguing fact: There is so much electromagnetic radiation occurring on and around the earth (microwave, radio, television, telephone, radar, and so on) that, if these signals were visible to the eye, earth would be the brightest "star" in the galaxy. All these signals are minute forces operating around, within, and upon us. When we consider all the other forces we experience, we must include the many workaday "pressures" we feel, the noise and clamor of the world, our various bodily functions, our thoughts, spiritual insights, passions, and the words we speak to each other. These all represent "forces" of some kind. What about love, antipathy, and hatred? The list of forces goes on and on. We cannot forget gravity, sunlight, the wind, and the rain—all the forces of nature.

There are books written about the many *inner* forces we seek to understand and to utilize. Golf pros would have their students master the "inner game" of golf before they actually tee off from a mound of grass somewhere. And whatever the outer forces may be, we all hope to muster sufficient inner force to stay "in control," to experience an inner sense of confidence and calm that balances the busyness and sometimes chaos of life to softly whisper, "My life is my own life to live."

In my consulting work, I sometimes help clients perform a Force Field Analysis, which is to look at the *Driving Forces* operating in favor of some intended outcome, as well as the *Restraining Forces* that will impede progress. The goal is to maximize the Driving Forces and minimize or eliminate the Restraining Forces. We want to "accentuate the positive and elimi-nate the negative," as the old song goes. We hope to get as many forces working in our favor as possible.

The "Receptive Force" Discovered

There are many intriguing philosophies—eastern and western—that help us examine the forces we can call upon that are part of the deeper or the divine nature we each possess. I recently read a very simple explanation of three inner forces labeled the *Active Force,* the *Receptive Force,* and the *Reconciling Force*. These labels immediately made sense to me in a very intuitive way that has been helpful. As you would surmise, the Active Force is the propensity we each have to *do*—to take action. The Receptive Force exists for the subtle purpose of simply assimilating what our amazing *senses* collect about the world around us. The Reconciling Force serves to bring our "action-oriented tendencies" together with our "sense of things" to create an overall awareness that helps us carry out *right actions*. Such reconciled actions are likely to be more complete and helpful than our initial inclinations to simply *do something*.

I have an abundance of the Active Force available to me. In some situations, I access it too readily. I am thankful for the Active Force, as there is plenty of action required to get through life and accomplish my goals. The third force or Reconciling Force rings of sensibility and reassurance to me. It is the middle force, the Receptive Force, that intrigues me most of all. It is the Receptive Force that draws the richness of the world and my experiences close around me so that there is genuine substance and sensitivity in my actions, and in any reconciliation I hope to accomplish. The more I contemplate the meaning of the Receptive Force, the more I am awed by the fact that my body is an amazing "receiver" of all the signals bombarding me, washing over me, and coming from within me.

To explain further, I must share with you the joy of solitude that is mine when I go for an Arizona desert walk. At first, the only signals I hear are the crunch, crunch of sand and gravel beneath my feet and the rush of thoughts inside my busy mind. Then, I decide to pause, to stop moving and clear my mind. I hear a bird singing, then dozens of birds singing, and then the wind in the Palo Verde trees. There are airplanes passing overhead. Sometimes, I will hear a pack of coyotes howling in the distance. I focus on the Saguaro cacti all around me. These bring back a boyhood connection with the desert—a spiritual connection that makes me feel protective of these magnificent monarchs of the desert. These saguaros are sacred to me.

At last, my mind is clear and no longer overactive. *It is receptive.* Now, I feel the gentle wind on my neck and on the back of my legs. I feel the slight weight of my fanny pack with its water bottles and other paraphernalia. Now, with each step I take, I enjoy the delightful sound of crunching sand and gravel. I am aware of the strength and agility I still possess. My mind is lifted to anticipate something of great importance. What is so important? It is whatever now flows into my mind. Perhaps it will be the voice of the cricket. At this point in my desert walk, I often pause again, look heavenward, and say to God, "I'm now open to suggestions, impressions, and any instructions you wish to give me. I have no questions and no agenda. I would be so thrilled and so thankful to have you whisper to me. If I know I am following your instructions, I will be content that all will be well, whatever the instructions may be. Thank you."

More Than a Meeting of the Minds

The Receptive Force is powerful in a business meeting. Next time you see the PowerPoint slides flashing and your associates turning the pages of their handouts, asking questions, attempting to influence, and jockeying for some prominence in the meeting, try this: Form a simple paragraph in your mind to frame the issues being discussed. Hold the thought briefly and then trust it to your subconscious mind or a notepad.

Now, take a long, slow, deep breath. Slide your chair back from the table slightly and relax a bit more into it—not so much that you appear to withdraw. Relax just enough to not feel caught up in the contest of ideas. Decide to not speak for a minute or so, whatever your inclinations to do so may be. Now, let your eyes move gently and randomly about the room to look at the face of each person there. Look long enough to not be intrusive or appear flirtatious, but to see the ears, the nose, the mouth, and the eyes of each person. Smile a very subtle smile of warmth as you do. Breathe deeply but slowly. Listen to the tone of each voice and not so much the words. Listen for the hum of the digital projector. Listen to the sliding of coffee mugs or the rustle of paper. Become aware of the up and down movement of your shoulders and chest as you breathe. Say to yourself:

I am surrounded by such interesting people who are so busy, so concerned. Some are eager to please and some are so eager to make things happen. There is an inner person for each person I see, each hoping to take the right actions. These people are just like me. I am so busy, so concerned, eager to please, and so eager to make things happen. I want to take the right actions. I hope we can each succeed. Somehow, we will need each other, though we may not realize it now. (Listen for a moment longer.) *When I speak again, I will speak a little more slowly than I typically do. I will continue breathing with the same steady rhythm. I will be calm. When I speak again, it will be to use my Reconciling Force. Then, as I continue to listen to the ideas others share, I will take notes. I will not react. I will not judge. I will thank others for the comments they make and ask for time to consider what I've heard.*

Mom, Are You Okay?

If you are a parent, you can do a version of this. You can leverage the receptive force in you to make life more relaxed and secure. Consider this: Amidst the rush of getting everybody off to school and work, stop and do the previous exercise with your own family. Decide that for a moment or two you will not speak or react to them. Observe them. Study their faces. What do you see in the expressions on their faces? Let your Receptive Force come to the foreground. As you do, your heart will rescue your frantic mind. Listening will replace speaking. Encouragement will replace criticism. From amidst the seeming chaos, you will gently pluck a moment of peace. You will remember who these people are. Suddenly, one of your children will stop, look you in the face, and ask, "Mom, are you okay?" You will reply, "I'm just listening to my family. I'm more than okay. Thanks."

The Receptive Force is the lever that opens the door to let in what the world is offering us so that we give back what the world needs. The insight we gain is the key to relevance. Relevance is extended leverage.

Leverage Key 16

Commitment

It was Christmas Eve. George's family would be sitting by the fire in their comfortable home. Tonight, George was crouched close to a small campfire that had been shielded with green boughs tied together and a deer hide slung over the top of the bundle. The wind was fierce. The sleet seemed to cut into the skin of George's face. His close friends confided their concerns about plans for Christmas Day.

At first, it appeared there would not be enough boats to carry all the men across the river. They must reach the other side in the middle hours between midnight and sunrise. Their surprise must be precisely executed and complete.

The wind grew stronger. George coughed and pulled his coat higher around his neck. Worry about

the boats had increased. He overheard some of the
men grumbling about their "miserable Christmas Eve."
George abruptly stood up. As he did, he knocked over
the crude windbreak that had protected the campfire. He looked from side to side at his men and then
declared, "This is a really bad night. Somebody forgot
to order enough boats. I don't feel that great. And I
miss my family. Quite frankly, I don't feel like crossing the Delaware tonight. Let's listen to our feelings.
Go back to your blankets and fires. We'll rethink this
whole thing about the Hessian troops in the morning.
The British will still be in New York City a day or
two from now. We have some bottles of ale. Pass them
around. Merry Christmas. It's the best we can do."

No Way!

Can you imagine George Washington not "feeling
like" crossing the Delaware, and therefore changing
his mind about his earlier commitment? No way. I
don't think so. As we discussed in Leverage Key 12
(Ownership and Stewardship), commitment is not a
feeling. It is not *about* feelings. It is about a decision
to move forward, often against the odds. It is about
the most glorious moment in our human adventure,
when individuals determine their destiny and perhaps
the destiny of all those who will follow them into the
future.

The initial group of colonial troops to cross the
Delaware numbered 2,500. After scattering the Hessian
troops and demolishing their resistance, Washington
knew he must seize the moment and forge on. He
needed a larger army. Pennsylvania Militiamen were
persuaded to extend their enlistments and to join his force.

Washington committed his own money to cover their pay. The force became 5,000 men strong.

Where Would You or I Have Stood?

The determination of one man moved colonists to become a nation. Not only did he meet his commitment to cross over and beyond the Delaware, he personally paid the troops to make it so. How committed was he? Where would you or I have stood that evening of December 24, 1776? Would we have stood firmly at his side, or slightly in the background waiting to discover how we felt about what was going on around us? It has always been said that there are those who make things happen, those who watch things happen, and those who wonder what happened. Where do you stand? Perhaps, if you or I could meet George Washington or Archimedes, they would be interested to know. One thing they would tell us: your commitment to do something is your ultimate leverage for getting it done.

So Let It Be Written

Commitment is not stubbornness. Stubbornness is usually unreasonable. Commitment is the result of thoughtful deliberation. It further leverages your core purpose and your self-determination. One of my favorite old movies is *The Ten Commandments* with Charlton Heston as Moses and Yul Bryner as Ramses, Pharaoh of Egypt. Moses is the hero; with God's help he did some fantastic things, most remarkably the parting of the Red Sea. Aside from the fact that Ramses gave the Children of Israel a really hard time, he did make a significant mark on history as the builder of great pyramids. Today's Egyptian tourism industry owes much to the early pharaohs. How much commitment would it take to part the Red Sea? Answer: A very strong commitment to the principles of faith. How much commitment would it take to build a pyramid? Answer: A very strong commitment to the principles of effective project management. There is one line in the movie for which we must give Ramses credit. It is his statement of commitment to his pyramid construction goals. He would say, "So let it be written, so let it be done." I like this statement. I sometimes abbreviate it as SLIBW-SLIBD. I make a personal commitment that once a goal is set, it is written. Once written, it becomes reality.

The Integrity of Your Vision

As for modern-day leaders, please consider the following questions that put the integrity of your vision to test as you make your commitments that lift the world.

1. What do I really believe about my organization's plans to "cross the Delaware"? Are my beliefs consistent with the effort that will be required? Are my beliefs that "I hope we can do it," or "I *know* it will happen"? What do I really believe about my people? Have I inherited some problem people? (A cop out) Am I experienced enough to rely on the great people I do have and to help those with "problems" be achievers?

2. Does my behavior leave open any excuses for others to do less than their best? Do my people see me talking, walking, interacting, recognizing, following through, and doing business with integrity in every sense of

the word? Are there any gaps between my statements and my behaviors? Where must I improve to be a better member of the team?

3. At the end of each day, what have I done to tangibly move our vision forward? In what ways have I specifically recognized any worthy effort by a member of my organization to do the same?

4. Do I listen with the ears of a detective and the heart of friend? Do I have the humility to seek advice and the courage to reject it from time to time? Is my decision process open to the input and influence of others, but my decisions unwavering once put to paper? So let it be written, so let it be done.

5. Realizing that small ideas and plans have no ability to inspire men and women, are mine BIG enough to inspire us all? Have I dared to undertake what some may consider to be "the impossible"? If not, am I merely going where others have gone before and doing what I have already done before?

6. Am I ready to break out and break through by joining forces with new partners to form radical alliances that will make the impossible *doable*? Who will I talk to this week whose creativity and capabilities we need?

7. Am I the kind of leader with whom capable and committed people would want to become partners?

8. What is the source of the vision I hold for the future? Is it merely a plausible wish for the future? Is it a determination to change the world? Guy Kawasaki did say, "You can be rich, you can be powerful, and you can be famous, but you won't amount to much of anything until you change the world."

9. What is my chief reason for wanting to, and deciding to change the world—my own Core Purpose? Is this purpose and the realization of the vision worth the effort that will be required? Why?

Commitment: A Magnificent Yet Tarnished Word

Commitment is a magnificent yet tarnished word. It is tarnished by its misuse, by those who speak of commitment, but whose hearts are not aligned with their words. My eldest son, Vance, who is a committed adventurer, told me of an intriguing book he's been reading, *Deep Survival: Who Lives, Who Dies, and Why,* by Laurence Gonzales. It contains amazing stories and fascinating research about survival and death in a variety of situations...many of these in the great outdoors. One of the book's most important conclusions that applies to our everyday lives is "It's not what's in your backpack that separates the quick from the dead. It's not even what's in your mind. Corny as it sounds, it's what's in your heart."

A true commitment is a magnificent act of courage. Such an act requires that your heart burn with a desire that feeds your passion and steels your determination. Then, what is imagined, hoped for, written about, or spoken *will be done*! The earth will move under your feet with such determination. The world will move upward in its orbit as you apply the unstoppable leverage of commitment.

Leverage Key 17

Agreement

I had just finished a seminar on "teamwork" at the Royal Aeronautical Society auditorium in London. A gentleman came to the front of the room and said, "Mr. Checketts, thank you for the seminar. I got just one thing out of it." In an instant, I agonized, "Just one thing—I guess it depends on what the one thing is." Before I could reply, my seminar student went on to say, "What I realized today is that our team needs to have more *conversations* and fewer meetings." Wow! I liked that. I thanked the gentleman and proceeded to ponder how to help teams have more and better conversations.

The result was a guidebook entitled *29 Questions That Will Energize Your Team*. I realized that much of what I had learned about teams during my career as a team member, team leader, and team consultant was this: Great teams learn to talk about what they may *need to* talk about *before* they *have to* talk about it.

As you reread the previous statement a couple of times you will discover its truth and the idea will catch on. Great teams learn to agree in principle on "who they are," what their mission is, and how they will handle difficulties and opportunities, *before* these actually occur. While ordinary teams will struggle with the surprises and crises they encounter, great teams will simply move from Plan A to Plan B and move forward.

Agreement in Principle

What power there is in *Agreement in Principle*. What power there is in *agreement*—period. *Agreement* is the extension of your *commitment* that will now include others on whom you depend and who depend on you. Once there is agreement, the management of relationships and outcomes becomes dramatically easier. Without agreement, management of anything is too often fuzzy, awkward, frustrating, and ineffective.

Consider the supervisor who is attempting to coach an employee who has failed to follow through on a customer commitment to schedule services on a timely basis.

Without an Agreement: "John, you need to be sure you take good notes when a customer calls and immediately enter these into the call log so that Margie can get a customer's service appointment scheduled with our field crews." Reply, "But I told her the customer called. She must have forgotten." "John, it's not her responsibility to pin down these customer commitments. It's yours. She just does the scheduling. You need to be sure to do your part here and don't leave others on the team hanging."

With an Agreement: "John, do you remember our agreement that you are responsible for making service call commitments to our customers and for entering these in to the call log so others can follow through with their responsibilities?" Reply, "Sure, I remember." "John, it appears this did not happen with the ACME account and we failed to have a field crew show up at the time you promised them. What do you think about this?" Reply: "I blew it, sorry." "Thanks, John, it is good that we track our agreements with each other and with each person on the team, isn't it?" "Yes, of course."

Without an agreement, it's about John and who's to blame. With an agreement, it's about the agreement and about fixing the problem.

Here is a parent-to-child example:

Without an Agreement: "Susan, I asked you to do the dishes and you just disappeared right after dinner. You need to learn to take more responsibility around the home."

With an Agreement: "Susan, we agreed that Monday, Wednesday, and Friday nights you would do the dishes right after dinner. What happened to that agreement?"

Messy or Easy? Confused or Clear?

The difference in both of the previous situations is that "with an agreement" meant the two parties had "talked about what they may need to talk about before they had to talk about it." Thus, their dialogue was "less personal," less messy, and far more effective. Ninety percent of management experts will help their clients discover that "you cannot manage people." People (young and old) will manage themselves. You can manage certain aspects of the work environment. You can create effective motivational strategies. But the greatest wisdom is that, while you cannot manage people, you can manage the agreements you have with people.

Next time you face a challenging relationship issue or a performance problem; consider one of these two conversations:

Without an agreement: "Darby, what is our agreement here? Oh, we don't have one do we. Let's discuss it. What would make sense as we commit to support each other? Once we agree, we can work together to track this agreement so we really support each other and get the job done. Sound good?"

With an agreement: "Darby, what did we agree about our responsibilities to each other in this situation? Have we met the agreement? What can we do to get the agreement back on track and keep it on track?"

Life Is Better With Commitment *and* Agreement

So let it be written, so let it be done works for you and me, as individuals. It also works for us, as a team. Life without agreements is similar to life without commitments. If you don't know where you're going, you will probably get nowhere. As you complete the aimless journey, you will waste valuable time and damage trust by trying to figure out who was to blame. Life with agreements is similar to life with commitments. You will reach your destination. As you complete your well-planned journey, you will be glad you and your fellow travelers had a basis for fixing the problems and not the blame.

To commit is to do.

To agree is the glue.

As I commit to myself,

I'll do the same for you.

Leverage Key 18

Thinking

My high school English teacher often reminded me that having a large and rich vocabulary of words would increase my potential for success in life, including a direct impact on the amount of money I would earn in my chosen profession. The idea sunk in. I already enjoyed reading. This vocabulary incentive was another contributor to what would become a lifelong love affair with words. Words are magic to me. In fact, they are the primary messengers that convey meaning from me to you and from you to me.

Sales Closer as a Navy Seal?

Many years after my English teacher taught me the value of words, I found myself in the role of a manufacturer's sales representative. My sales manager was a seasoned salesman, a real go-getter who was considered to be a "super closer." As a new sales rep, I considered a "super closer" to be the sales equivalent of a Navy Seal. So, when the closer spoke, I listened. One day, as we were driving to our next sales appointment, he said to me, "Darby, the secret to success in selling is to have a rich vocabulary of patterns." I puzzled, "Vocabulary of patterns—hmmm—I wonder how you get one of those." My sales manager went on to explain that on one hand, a *mere salesman* attempts to sell a product. On the other hand, a world-class salesperson recognizes a pattern of customer needs and then weaves the product's features together to create a distinctive solution for each customer's unique situation. The more patterns he could see and weave, the more sales he would make. Aha!

A Rich Vocabulary of Patterns

In subsequent years, I have worked on my vocabulary of patterns and enjoyed observing others who possessed world-class problem-solving *and* selling skills. My sales manager had done more than introduce me to two concepts of "vocabulary"; he had made it even clearer to me that there are multiple and distinct dimensions of thinking about life's problems and their solutions.

What Do You Think About Thinking?

I believe that for much of my life I must have thought what most people think about "thinking"—not much at all. We take it for granted. We do not receive any formal instruction on "how to operate a brain." We just do it. *Thinking* is some generalized thing that just happens when you wake up in the morning, your brain turns on, and you face the world. We all hope our thinking is equal to the task. Often, whatever thoughts we get, we are satisfied with, we sort of go with the flow. Perhaps we should think of the human brain as if it were an automobile that you can climb into and drive anywhere you wish, on varying terrain, shifting into four-wheel drive for off-road, and back into overdrive for zooming down the highway. Actually, books such as this one are owner's manuals for successfully operating your brain. Let me invite you to consider the instructions below, rev up your brain, and take a test drive. Try some scenic highways or mountain roads you may not have driven before.

Drive Your Brain on the Autobahn of Life

Over the years, I have worked to help our clients think multi dimensionally about their customer's needs so they could seize all the opportunities to move to the new world I call "Customer Astonishment." The following conceptual model is based on my early research that began in 1991. About six years ago, the Capital Development Board of the State of Illinois asked me to address this very unique conference theme: "Thinking Bigger and Better." I was so impressed that this group was visionary enough to address the bedrock fundamentals of thinking that most of us tend to overlook. It turns out that the principles of *effective thinking* are the underpinnings of the Customer Astonishment model I have used with my clients for nearly 15 years. Here is the model, as further instructions on how to operate the marvelous brain we have each been given.

	Present Situations	Future Situations
To Sense	Think AHEAD *Be Receptive* Anticipate Q1	Think BEYOND *Be Inspired* Envision Q2
To Know	Think ABOUT *Be Aware* Understand Q3	Think BIG *Be Bold* Strategize Q4

Let's discuss the 2 x 2 dimensions that define the four quadrants of this grid. The vertical dimension is about the difference between operating out of your conscious mind—*knowing*—versus operating out of your subconscious mind—*sensing*. The horizontal dimension is simply about "the here and now" versus what may happen at some future time.

When you *know* something in the *present* (Q1), you think *about* what actually is. Your conscious mind is giving you visual, auditory, and other tangible cues about the situation. As you expand your *awareness*, you seek to *understand*.

When you *sense* something in the *present* (Q2), you instinctively realize there is more to the situation than meets the eye or the ear. As you are *receptive* to the more subtle input from the environment that surrounds you, you will respond to situations with heightened sensitivity. You will think *ahead* to *anticipate* what's about to come next.

Speaking in terms of human communication, and to illustrate the interaction between Quadrants 1 and 3, your conscious mind (Q1) picks up the verbal cues, while your subconscious mind (Q2) picks up nonverbal cues. For example, imagine you are having a conversation with someone you love. Your companion's words may be telling you one thing, but somehow "the look" on his or her face is telling you something else. You may think to reply with words then suddenly realize that a hug will have far more meaning in this situation.

When you *know* something is likely to happen in the *future* that will represent an opportunity or a challenge (Q3), you have time to prepare for the upcoming event. You could shrink from the challenge and avoid the situation or think *big* and rise to the occasion. As you develop *a strategy* for expanding your capabilities, you can be more *bold* and move forward with full readiness.

When you *sense* something is likely to happen in the *future* (Q4), some will consider you to be clairvoyant or just plain "nuts." You are thinking *Beyond* the norm. If you figure you *are* "losing it" and going nuts (I think not), you should seek help. If you are confident, you're not nuts, and feel *inspired*, smile to yourself and *envision* your future success. As you do, you will realize that (a) you *are* a genius in your own right and (b) you are seeing things in a brand new pattern that others may be missing. Perhaps you are about to become the next Jeff Bezos of *Amazon.com*, or one of his good friends, J.K. Rowling, author of the Harry Potter books.

Bezos, Rowling, and You

Mr. Bezos and Ms. Rowling have been doing two things we've been talking about very well: (1) operating their brains with skill by utilizing multiple dimensions of thinking, and (2) cultivating a rich vocabulary of patterns based on studying the future and paying attention to their intuitions. Congratulations to them. What is especially exciting is that you and I can do the same thing. You may not revolutionize the retailing industry via the Internet or become a billionaire best-selling author, but you will move to the next level of whatever you're now doing and expand your potential for success, wealth, and happiness significantly. Trust your intuition and your inspiration. Have the courage to follow it. You absolutely do have creative and powerful thoughts!

Your Interplanetary Test Drive

Are you ready for a test drive of that super car just under your scalp? Given that you are reading this book, your brain is already turned on and running smoothly. I hope you agree. Okay, now go nuts. Start with this exercise. Grab a pen and a notepad or use your computer keyboard to jot down ideas in response to this mental challenge: In the next 90 seconds, write down all the reasons you can think of: *why the human race should send representatives to the planet Mars*. Go.

Stop. Okay, you're warmed up. Now, do another 90 seconds, but specifically address three categories:

1. Identify several serious benefits that will result from our journeys to Mars.

2. Be *bold* and propose several "Sci-Fi" reasons for going to Mars that are way beyond high-tech, and beyond any extreme adventures possible here on earth.

3. Finally, dare to be a comic and propose at least one totally outrageous reason for going to Mars. Laugh, but then don't laugh.

Somebody's going there for just such a reason. It's only a matter of time.

This Mars question is a fun question with serious, intriguing, and hilarious implications. Did you address the three categories above? Did your list of reasons to go to Mars expand? If your list is exploding…if you're going "woo-ooh-woo" about the sci-fi stuff and you're laughing at your own outlandish humor…*great*! If not, you need to find a friend or work associate to join you and challenge your thinking or give you permission to turn on the creativity.

Back to Your World

Now, think just as creatively as you answer the following questions about your own world, right here on earth.

1. Where is your biggest mental rut…a no longer helpful mode of thinking that is holding you back? Is it time to drive your brain right around this rut and out onto the open road? How? What will be your new thinking habit to replace the old? This book should hold some "keys" to start the engine.

2. Where is your safest, most well-fortified harbor…something about you that makes you feel confident in yourself and in the future? Build on this. Another mentor of mine once said, "Success is figuring out what you do really well and doing a lot of it."

3. Which is your tallest mountain to climb in life…perhaps a serious challenge you will face in the not-too-distant future? How will you prepare? Once you reach the astronomical observatory on top of the mountain,

what will you see out there in the galaxy beyond Mars?

4. Which is *your* brightest star…that sometimes hidden talent waiting to burst forth and help you open new doors?

5. What pieces of the puzzle of life and its many problems and opportunities do you possess that could form the pattern of a revolutionary breakthrough for you and those around you—your best-selling book, a product invention, or a creative idea for addressing a major challenge facing your own family or community?

Next time you face a situation, a challenge, or an opportunity in life, consider at least four dimensions of thinking, just as you would come to an intersection while driving your car and recognize four distinct directions you can steer. Think clearly *about* the "here and now" of your life. Think just *ahead* about current situations to recognize what else is going on that you may be overlooking. Think *big* about what you are capable of becoming and doing, given the time you have to prepare and to discover new resources. Think *beyond* where you may otherwise limit your creativity, or where others are afraid to go and where breakthroughs may await you. The human mind is a lever with amazing power to lift you and the world.

Leverage Key 19

Learning

"Will America Slip from No. 1?" This is the title of an editorial by David Gergen, Editor at Large for *U.S.News & World Report*. Mr. Gergen's chief concern is the quality of education in America. He cited a landmark national education commission report, which concluded that our nation's schools face a "rising tide of mediocrity." On a list of 20 developed nations, America currently ranks 16th in high school graduation rates and 14th in college graduation rates. Mr. Gergen pointed out that Bill Gates is among a growing number of CEOs who are very concerned. Mr. Gates told a group of governors, "I am terrified for our workforce of tomorrow." Many university presidents and corporate CEOs feel the urgent need to rally Washington and the country to a revolutionary overhaul of public education. Americans have generally been among the most literate people on Earth and this fact put us on an ever-upward path. Now, this leverage is at risk.

Education: The Greatest Hope for a Bright Future

This Leverage Key is about education and the vital importance of lifelong learning. It is also aimed primarily at young people for whom formal education is the greatest hope they have for a bright future. With all this in mind, there is no greater contribution to the health of our society than that which is made by community leaders, teachers, and parents who help our youth discover the joy of learning. Use this key to enlighten and inspire the youth you know.

Young Archimedes Learns

A Parable. Young Archimedes was awakened from a deep sleep by the bright light that suddenly filled his bedroom. In the midst of the light, he thought he saw a child-like fairy, or perhaps an angel who softly spoke these words:

My young friend, don't be frightened. Mine is the face of your future. It is bright and full of hope. I have come to give you these instructions. You are now eight years old. Since you were a tiny boy, you have dreamed of climbing the sacred mountain that lies at the end of the beautiful valley you call home. Until now, you have been too young for such an adventure. Two years ago, your father thought of carrying you up the mountain, but he has grown older and even the weight of a small boy would be too great a burden. You have become strong. You are no longer afraid of the darkness. With me to guide you, you can now make the journey on your own. Tonight I will tell you why this dream of the mountain has been so vivid inside your young mind.

On the mountaintop, there is a very young tree, a sapling. It is also eight years old. The sapling is seven feet tall and very sturdy. It grows for one purpose alone: to become a staff for you to use on a long journey to accomplish the greatest feats of your life. Young man, are you ready to go to the mountain?" Archimedes inquired, "Tonight, must we begin tonight?" The angel went on, "Not tonight, but tomorrow morning when the sky is first light and the sun is still behind the hilltops. Bring with you bread, cheese, fruit, water, and the small saw that hangs near the door in your father's tool shed. Bring your cloak. Tell no one of your destination, but write a note to your beloved parents to comfort them in your absence. Tell them that you are in the company of an angel who will protect you and who must lead you to discover your future. Place this golden key on top of your note. They will have never seen one like it before and will know that it is a sign of my power to protect you."

Young Archimedes had never walked so far from his home before. The other end of the valley came closer and closer. He could see the beautiful green mountain the people of his village believed to be so sacred. The angel had disappeared from his view, but, inside his mind, the angel continued to speak with a soft voice of reassurance that guided his footsteps. He was led to a beautiful clearing at the foot of the mountain.

On the opposite side of the clearing was a pathway that led up the mountain. At times, the path was easy, the birds sang in the trees, and sunlight glistened through their branches. Then, suddenly, his way would become dark as clouds blocked the sun and the trees appeared to grow together around him. As the path became steeper, rocks were more prevalent and he would sometimes climb with hand and foot to keep his balance.

By the mid-afternoon as the sun was setting in the west toward his home, he could see the top of the mountain. Now the angel spoke very clearly in his mind's ear and said:

"Watch for a sapling that grows at the side of the pathway and leans just slightly across it, as if to stop you in your tracks. A small bird will be sitting in its branches and will call your name. As you approach, the bird will fly away. Hold the tree in your hands. Say a prayer of thanksgiving for the strength it will provide you on your life's journey ahead. Take your saw and gently cut it down making sure the cut is straight and clean. In the same manner, cut all the small branches from the sapling. When you are done, sit and rest briefly. As you sit, finish the bread, the cheese, and the fruit in your knapsack. Prepare for your journey home. Then, whistle as you walk. Your new staff will bring you joy. But helping you walk down the mountain slope is its secondary purpose. Its true purpose will be revealed as you travel along. You will meet others on your way who will need your help. Befriend them and do what you can to assist them."

As Archimedes walked back toward the valley below, he met others from the village who had come to the mountain as well. At one bend in the trail homeward, a few people had gathered. They were anxiously shouting and moving about, trying to help a small boy who lay at the side of the path. As Archimedes approached, he could see that the boy's leg was wedged under a small boulder. He asked what had happened. "He slid off the path and his leg entered a rabbit's burrow under this rock. The rock settled and we can't move it yet. Can you use your staff to lift it up so we can pull him out?" Archimedes was eager to help. He placed the staff under the rock and easily tilted it upward. The frightened boy was freed. His leg was unbroken. Just a boy himself, Archimedes had come along to save the day...and then slipped quietly on his way. As he reentered the valley at the foot of the mountain, he came upon an old woman working to free her three cows from inside a gate, so she could lead them home for milking. The gate was stuck. She saw the boy and beckoned for help with her cows. Archimedes went to her and said, "Please stand back, I'll pry the gate open with my staff," which he did.

Just as Archimedes could see his home in the distance, a small girl came running toward him. She cried out, "Boy, my scarf was caught by the wind. It's hanging up in that tree. Can you reach it?" With his arms stretched to the limit and holding the staff high up in the air, Archimedes pricked the edge of the scarf and gently tugged it from the branches. It fell to the ground. The little girl picked it up, quickly hugged him, and ran happily on her way. What a day this had been for an eight-year-old boy, indeed.

As the summer sun sank behind the hilltops, Archimedes entered the front gate of his home. His parents rushed to greet him. "Son, we were not worried.

We knew you were safe. What did you discover? And by the way, we've heard stories of a boy who helped many townspeople today. They said he was strong beyond his years. Was it you?" "Yes, mother and father, I think I am the boy they spoke of. But I confess that this strength is not my own. It was given to me by an angel. It's in the form of this staff that you see. With it, I can lift things, pry things open, reach high in the sky, and scare away the fierce dogs. And I lean on it when I'm tired. Poppa, what is its secret?" "My son, it is a lever. You have used small sticks to pry stones from the ground and chase rats from the chicken coop. Now, you have a larger stick. It is so straight and smooth. Carve your initials upon it. Keep it always. With this staff you could lift the world." "Thank you, Poppa, I will keep it all of my life." "One more thing, dear son, to know all the ways you can use it; you must study and learn each day at the village school where we send you. Your teacher knows of wheels and ropes and pulleys and levers and the fulcrums you use with these, and the many other tools that help grown-ups with their work. One day, you will be the master of these tools and teach others. Perhaps you *will* lift the world."

Each Child Must Climb the Mountain

Each child in this world must climb to the top of a mountain to find the lever that will give them strength beyond their own. Their teachers are the angels who will guide them on their way. To climb the mountain is to finish school. They must keep the mountain peak in view and not grow weary from the journey. From the top of the mountain, they will see a panorama of opportunities they could never see before. Their triumph will be well worth the effort. The sapling they cut down will be the education they gain. It will give them *Leverage*. It will be the tool they need to move boulders, open gates, and reach their dreams.

Leverage Key 20

Mechanisms

One of my favorite and most influential business books of all time is *Built to Last*, by Jim Collins and Jerry Porras. In it, they identified the leadership qualities and contributions that have the most significant and lasting impact. The book illustrated the importance of "clock building" versus merely "telling time." Although some would consider charisma to be an important leadership trait, it is far down the list of "high impact" leadership qualities. Collins and Porras proclaimed that a high profile, charismatic leadership style is absolutely not required to successfully shape a visionary company. The most important contribution the greatest leaders make is to create *Mechanisms*. In this context, the company is a far greater creation than the products it sells. The company is the tree that bears the fruit. The authors concluded, "We suggest that the continual stream of great products and services from highly visionary companies stem from them being outstanding organizations, not the other way around."

A mechanism can be defined as: *The means by which an effect is produced or a purpose is accomplished and whereby this effect or accomplishment can be easily replicated. We acknowledge the means apart from the "accomplishment" itself.* We seize upon, use, and benefit from the *means*. It is leverage on both our effectiveness and our efficiency.

Consider the following examples of high-impact mechanisms:

- ✓ **United States Constitution.** Far greater than the leadership of George Washington, Thomas Jefferson, and the founding fathers of our country was their creation of the United States Constitution. These visionary leaders built a clock that would keep on ticking through the ages. They set in motion principles that would steadily guide a nation long after they were gone. A single written document would become leverage on a million decisions we would face as a nation. This document would become the key to leveraging democracy around the world.

- ✓ **The Internet and *Amazon.com*.** The Internet may be the most influential mechanism of our modern age. Jeff Bezos is the visionary leader who built upon this pervasive medium to perfect the mechanisms of online merchandising. It isn't what Amazon sells that is distinctive; it is the process they have designed that is this company's legacy. I am sure Mr. Bezos is a very impressive individual, possessed of much knowledge and a true fountain of ideas and energy. However, his greatest accomplishment is that he can take a long vacation while the books, CDs, and a world of other products get ordered with a click, get billed to our Visa accounts with a click, are sent down a conveyor belt, boxed, and loaded onto a delivery truck for shipment to our doorsteps a day or two earlier than promised. Is the Amazon process as a lever lifting a huge boulder or two? The Amazon lever moves a zillion products around the globe and leverages the financial capital of the corporation by eliminating the need for many physical and human assets otherwise required by a conventional product retailer.

√ **Air Conditioning.** William Haviland Carrier is considered to be the "Father of Cool." Aren't we glad? He built upon the work of other inventors to make "refrigeration" a practical mechanism for cooling your home. Consider the immense leverage of this technology. There are hot and humid regions of the globe that would be so uninviting as to be almost uninhabitable without air conditioning. I live in the beautiful Sonoran Desert of Arizona and love my lifestyle here. However, without Mr. Carrier's mechanism, I would soon sell my home and move to Colorado.

✓ Seven Habits. One of the best-selling business and self-help authors of all time is Stephen Covey. His famous "7 Habits" are a mechanism for taking control of your life and making your success more predictable. Long after Mr. Covey is gone, his books will be sitting on desks and tables as a resource for millions of readers.

These mechanisms are also a legacy for their creators, but they are more than this. A legacy brings a sense of contribution along with certain honors. However, these mechanisms we have been speaking of here are the *Grand Tools* that others use to leverage their day-to-day activities for greater efficiency and effectiveness. Without these mechanisms or tools, we would still be digging in our backyard gardens with a sharp stick to plant some seeds and hope for food in the months ahead.

Mechanisms: Your Creations

Your Mechanisms: Any "principle and practice" of organization and personal effectiveness you create serves you as a mechanism of success. Without such mechanisms, you leave everything to chance. Without these, everything you do is a random act. When your mechanisms of success become internalized as simply "the way you do things," these have become habits. Habits are the most personal form of mechanisms. Many of the "keys" discussed in this book are the basis for creating new and especially helpful habits. As you consciously develop these habits, you will seize upon the Archimedes Factor again and again as you leverage your personal power and effectiveness. Furthermore, as you and your team identify "core values" or certain "principles of team conduct," these become mechanisms to make productive behaviors more predictable.

Be a creator of mechanisms. These outlast the "things" you do. These can be documented, diagrammed, illustrated, and passed on to others. Your leadership will have a truly long-lasting impact. Here is a mechanism for creating mechanisms:

1. Find a need.

2. Create a solution to fill the need.

3. Test it to be sure it works reliably and satisfies a majority of those who would use it.

4. Figure out how to make it as easy to use as possible so the product or procedure is not dependent on you.

5. Document what you have created and determine how to teach others to understand and use the product or procedure.

6. If you simply intend to help others perform more efficiently and effectively, count your success and move on to creating the next mechanism. We thank you for building a clock and helping others to   tell time rather than their becoming dependent on you to know the time of day.

7. If you have just discovered the newest secrets of air conditioning or online product marketing, write a business plan and leverage all the resources you can find to make a BIG dream come true. If you have just identified the 10th or 11th habit of highly effective people, write a book. If you have a proposed amendment to the United States Constitution, write your representatives in Congress, or enroll in law school to become one.

If this book has prompted you to cultivate a new Archimedes habit that represents greater leverage for life and leadership, *so let it be written, so let it be done.*

Leverage Key 21

Partnerships

The mechanisms we explored in Leverage Key 20 were the physical tools and processes we devise to help with the tasks set before us. Beyond these, there is a "Mechanism of All Mechanisms." It is the very human mechanism we call *Partnership*. Accompanied by the force of human desire that propels us forward, our partnerships with others are likely to be our most powerful mechanisms. I firmly believe that nothing is impossible with the right partnerships.

Powerful Leverage: Right There Under My Nose

Just a few years ago, two of our most important clients asked if our company could provide Web-based learning programs to complement our "live" training curriculum. Such programs were coming into view and I felt we must oblige these clients. I knew we did not have the appropriate computer servers to host such courses nor the software sophistication to enroll students and keep the records required for college credit. At the same time, I do try hard to practice what I preach and emphasize the "can do." I told my clients I needed a little time to check on the possibilities and I would get back to them with a plan.

That afternoon as I was traveling along the Red Mountain Freeway on my way home, I found myself very perplexed by the seemingly impossible requirement to get Web-based training up and running without more resources. As a bolt out of the blue, I suddenly (and fortunately) remembered that I had just completed our "Customer Astonishment" training for nearly all the employees of Rio Salado College of Tempe, Arizona. I wondered if the college could partner with us to create and deliver our new online training programs.

When I got back to my office, I called Dr. Linda Thor, President of Rio Salado, and simply said, "Linda, I need to put our Customer Astonishment training out there on the Web. Can you help me?" Dr. Thor is an exceptionally entrepreneurial college president, from my experience. She said, "Sure, we can help. How about you create the course and we'll put it on our computers. You will be responsible for all content support and we'll take care of the technical support." I asked about the financial side of things. Her reply, "You handle your front-end costs; we'll handle ours, and how about we split the revenue 50/50?" I asked, "Do we need some sort of a contract?" She said, "Send me an e-mail. When you're in the office next, we'll shake on it." Six months later, our company had a full-blown Web-based training program up and running.

Wow! What power the right partnerships can represent. I went from intimidated, to over my head, to having a fantastic community college in my hip pocket to help me serve my customers. I congratulated myself on waking up to the incredible resource Rio Salado College represented, right there under my nose. I thank Linda Thor for her all-around enthusiasm and "make it happen" attitude.

Nothing Is Impossible

Others come to me and say, "We have to do the impossible." I consistently reply, "Nothing is impossible. You just haven't found all of the right partners yet. And by the way, congratulations on *thinking* B-I-G." The problem is we tend to look for partners in all the right places. You've got to look in the *wrong* places, where others may not look and where you might least expect to find the partners you need. The best partners often represent the "odd couple" arrangement that proves to be pure magic because each partner somehow helps the other break out and break through. Here are some key criteria for your new millennium partners in business or other arenas of your life. These partners...

- ✓ May scare you at first—by challenging your thinking and your traditions—and yet somehow they resonate to your core purpose.
- ✓ Quite possibly compete with you in some aspect of your business, if not directly.

✓ Do some of the same things you do in a totally different way.

✓ Possess certain capabilities that *do* complement your own capabilities.

✓ Travel in circles you do not.

✓ Utilize marketing and distribution channels you may have overlooked or rejected.

✓ Possess a piece of the puzzle you've been missing.

How far out of your comfort zone are you prepared to go to find the partners you need? Be fearless in choosing your partners. Form radical alliances.

The Great Wisdom of Partnerships

The most profound achievers set goals beyond the power of a single person to achieve. Build the Hoover Dam. Put a man on the moon. Cure cancer. End poverty. Such leaders use leverage to extend their power and do the impossible. Their accomplishments are monumental. They see no conflict between the important concept of self-determination and the need to find the best tools or the deepest pools of talent to draw upon. If there were any inkling that another person might possess the missing ingredient in a complex recipe for success, that person would soon become a partner. Then, when triumph occurs, the achiever is admired for being both personally powerful and also wise enough to choose exceptional partners.

"Partnerships" may be about your business or some other enterprise. They may be about moving forward with your personal or career goals. Some of these partners are mentors and door openers. Let me tell you of such a great partner. Gene Mondani was my boss at Digital Equipment Corporation a number of years ago. We have remained close friends in all the years since. At the time we met, I was a member of the Sales Training department at DEC, doing my training thing and building on my sales background. I was always looking for new breakthroughs. Somehow, Gene became aware of my reputation as an effective trainer and invited me to his office. He was the Corporate Manager of Quality Assurance and reported to the Vice President of Manufacturing. His staff of quality engineers was responsible for quality company-wide that included supporting Digital's rapidly growing number of manufacturing plants.

Gene began our get-acquainted interview with a test question. He said, "Young man, have you ever had a real job? Would you be interested in working in the *real* world of manufacturing?" I reserved judgment about his opening remark and took it with the good humor he also intended. My reply was simply, "What do you have in mind?" He went on to say that he had plenty of good, technically qualified engineers, but needed someone to explain "quality assurance" to everybody involved, in nontechnical terms they could understand. He said he had heard that I was a good communicator, and that's what he needed.

Working for Gene Mondani was one of the highlights of my life, and the role I played in Corporate Quality Assurance proved to be a significant broadening and balancing factor in my overall career experience. Gene and I forged the intellectual and sometimes political partnership necessary to drive quality initiatives across our company's many and diverse organizations— some supportive, some not. We also developed a partnership of the spirit that I can best illustrate with the following story.

Partnership in Living Color

At one of our management meetings, I happened to be giving a presentation. Gene sat next to a very important senior manager whose support we needed. As I was speaking, I overheard this fellow ask Gene, "How come you so often let Darby give the presentations in these big meetings?" Whew! I needed to hear the rest of this conversation. You see, I was about 33 years old and very new to the organization. Gene's response would be very important to me.

Gene leaned over to his friend and said, "I let Darby give these presentations because he's better at it than I am, *but I hired Darby.*" He said these last words with considerable emphasis. Gene always let me get the credit for what I accomplished. On the other hand, he took credit for being the genius that hired and coached me. Gene's partnership was invaluable in getting so much done. In an age before the phrase "got your back" was coined, we did cover each other's backs. Ours was a very complementary professional relationship. I am grateful that Gene saw my potential, and that I had the good sense to join his team.

Cultivating great partnerships is an art form. Learn it. Master it. Enjoy it. The process begins with, and is guided by these insights, which may seem obvious, but about which you and I can generally use a good reminder.

1. It is impossible for one person or one business entity to know all, see all, hear all, discover all, or in any way do all that is needed. This means that any assumption to "go it alone" without partners is to do so with many voids of knowledge, expertise, and

leverage. How much are you willing to risk by going it alone?

2. As Ralph Waldo Emerson said, "Every person I meet is in some way my superior and in that I can learn from him (or her)." The greatest wisdom of all is to seek the wisdom of others.

3. Some of those who become your partners (mentors, coaches, allies, door openers, and so on) will often give you a swift kick in the direction of your potential. One day you'll be very glad they did, if not at first.

4. When you finally stand in the winner's circle of life, be sure to turn to the crowd and say, "I have great partners and fantastic alliances that make the impossible possible. I acknowledge and thank them."

Although all the levers of life have distinct merits, a good partnership is most likely the longest lever of all when the task before you is monumental. Expand your partnerships.

Leverage Key 22

Money and Wealth

Is it true that money *can't* buy you happiness? Or is it true that with enough money you can get anything you want in this world? With plenty of money, think about what you can do. If you're sick, you can hire the best doctors. If you are bored, you can buy a Ferrari and drive it on the autobahn. If you're too busy, you can hire two or three assistants. If you feel blue or depressed, you can hire a therapist or escape to the mountains of Tibet for self-discovery. And money is leverage, right? You can change the world with money. You can start a business that provides jobs for others while you build your net worth. One day, you can donate millions to help provide housing for hundreds of families. When you retire in luxury, you will do so with a great sense of satisfaction. Isn't it incredible what money can do?

No, it is incredible what *you* can do with money. By the way, money itself is not leverage and it is also true that money cannot buy happiness. The fact is money can do nothing. It is what you and I do with money, based on the real leverage our desires and dreams represent, that matters. The leverage we associate with money is tied to all the other keys we have previously discussed. With money you *can* acquire some of the mechanisms you need to achieve your goals. If the things you do with money lift the world, this will contribute to your happiness. Finally, there is an important distinction between the ideas of *being rich* (merely possessing lots of money) and *being wealthy* (possessing assets of lasting value).

What We Think About Money

It is what you and I *think* about money that makes all the difference—most of us spend a lot of time thinking about money. For some, it's a matter of scraping up enough money (or its equivalent) to survive. For others, it's about keeping score and perhaps responding to the challenge: "He who dies with the most toys wins." I picked up many of my perceptions about money from life with my dad. He was self-employed for most of his life. It took much self-confidence and self-determination to provide for a family the way he did. Whatever his formal titles may have been, he was essentially a salesman and it seemed that we all lived from commission check to commission check. My dear dad always seemed to be in search of more money. My perception was that we had what we needed as a family *in the present* and yet we were always unsure about an adequate supply of money in the future. I remember kneeling with my mother and siblings to pray fervently that dad would be able to make a sale *today*...because we needed the money for some big expense that lay on the near horizon.

Jim Carrey and Me

As a boy, I came to think of money as nice to have, but a big worry. For some, this would have resulted in a determination to become rich to be able to stop worrying about money. I remember reading about actor Jim Carrey whose dad was too often on the short side of money. This caused the skillful funnyman, Jim, to become obsessed with the need to be financially independent, even rich. The effects of my boyhood perceptions of money were nearly the opposite for me. I decided that lots of other stuff was more important than money and that I would pursue these things in earnest and trust the "get enough money" thing to be a natural byproduct of my diligence.

This perception of money has been both a blessing and a fallacy. The blessing has been that I have never obsessed about money and my priorities have seemed to be appropriate around what we all know really matters in life. I (we) have lived through poor times and not-so-poor times and managed to stay happy in spite of the presence or absence of money. This is a blessing. The fallacy was, for some time, I did not place enough emphasis on building wealth for all the right reasons—to acquire additional mechanisms and create the broadest opportunities to do my dreams and lift the world. I might have looked upon Jim Carrey as being too mercenary and yet I am awed by the financial resources he can bring to bear on whatever worthy goals he may choose.

True Grit

With all of the financial challenges my dad faced, he certainly did develop one personal characteristic of value that those who are born rich (or who acquire riches easily) may never get the opportunity to develop. My dad possessed "true grit" when it came to being self-reliant. When the financial chips were down, he simply worked harder and became more determined to find money somewhere. He often worked miracles to "make that sale" just in time to keep our family's financial ship afloat. I am thankful to say that my dad did pass along a good deal of his "true grit" to me. He taught me to work, as good dads generally do. He taught me to be self-reliant and to be resourceful. As my own 20 years of self-employment can attest, these attributes can be as valuable as gold in the vault.

100 Bucks for Four Years of College

At the point in time when I was to set off for college, my dad was having an especially difficult time in business. He apologized that he would not be much help to me financially. We lived in Hilo, Hawaii, and I would be going to college on the mainland, so my travel and other expenses would be considerable. I vividly remember the drive to the Hilo, Hawaii airport knowing that I was now officially leaving home and would soon be on my own. After we parked the car, my mother with tears in her eyes and my dad in his brightest aloha shirt accompanied me to the edge of the tarmac (in the days before air conditioned airline boarding ramps). My mother hugged me. Then, my dad pulled me aside as he pulled out his billfold. He handed me a crisp, new 100-dollar bill and said, "Son, this is for college, $25 for each of the four years. Spend it wisely." He was completely serious and I knew it. (That was the last money I ever received from my parents.) So, what was I to do?

As I walked slowly toward the airplane, I must admit that fear crept in. Then, I recounted the things my dad had taught me about hard work and self-reliance. I was blessed with a healthy body and a sound mind, which were the basis for a high level of self-confidence. So, the answer to the question of what I needed to do in my new independent situation with not much more than $100 cash to my name was suddenly clear. As I contemplated who I had been taught to be and climbed the stairs to the open aircraft door above me, the fear subsided. I boarded the flight to my future with a determination to be self-reliant and never looked back. I knew that I would somehow find the money I needed. I was also firmly resolved that my happiness would not depend on money.

Years later as I started my own business and became self-employed, other aspiring entrepreneurs would ask me what it was all about and what they needed to be and do to successfully venture forth on their own. One of my answers has been, "You must be prepared to lose everything financially and materially, but to realize you have lost nothing of true significance, and then be able to start all over again with just $100 in your pocket."

Okay, Who's the Funniest Guy?

Beyond the fact that Jim Carrey is a slightly funnier guy than me, I assume there are today several fundamental differences between him and me when it comes to money.

1. I am sure he has obsessed over money more than I have.
2. He is far richer than I am.
3. There is a good chance he has had more fun than me (as in "having a blast").
4. I doubt he has experienced any more joy than I have.

Today, as I write this chapter of the book, our 19th grandchild has been born. Two days ago, our youngest son, Matt, proposed to his true love. I am sitting in an airplane at 32,000 feet on my way home from Alaska and a very successful consulting engagement with a favorite client, Alaska Interstate Construction. My suitcase is full of freshly caught Alaskan salmon, halibut, and rockfish. My sweetheart and wife of nearly 40 years will soon be meeting me at the Phoenix airport. It's the Fourth of July weekend and I am proud to be an American. God is watching over me. I have my health. Life is good. I am a very wealthy man, indeed.

Let's Have a Blast, Jim

Personal Note to Jim Carrey: Jim, if you read this book and I'm wrong about you, please give me a telephone call. We'll swap stories about our dads. You can buy me a sumptuous dinner somewhere in Beverly Hills and I'll bring just a few photos of my grandkids. We'll have a blast.

What to Do About Money

So, what is my advice about money? One of my wise friends once said, "Pray that your family is neither rich nor poor." Another friend once told me, "We've been rich and we've been poor and rich is better." *So, what's the answer for heaven's sake?*

Maximize your professional skills and investment know-how so that your time and efforts are highly leveraged to provide you with meaningful experiences and the opportunity to accumulate wealth. Never let the wealth become the end, but a means to worthy ends you will choose to serve. Spend sufficient money to meet the needs of those you love and to have some fun. Do not turn your back on those in need. Decide that there is absolutely not enough money in the world to ever convince you to compromise what you stand for or the agreements you have with those who love and trust you. If you were to ever make such a compromise, you would lose the wealth money cannot buy and die a spiritual pauper. Prepare for the day when you will have the joy of using your wealth to make the world a far better place. This joy will be the best return on any financial investment you have ever made.

To conclude, here are three proven principles to help you acquire and manage the money you need to create the true wealth you really want.

   ✓ Rule #1: Perspective and Control. Keep money in perspective as a *means*, not an end. You control it so that its scarcity *or* abundance never controls you.

   ✓ Rule #2: Consistency Over Time. Consistently put a definite portion of money in the right places...over time. And, the earlier you start and the more you study your options (right places), the better you'll do.

   ✓ Rule #3: Value, Value, Value. In the economic enterprise of life, deliver true value for those who support, reward, and depend on you. Know the significant value of what you create and don't be afraid to price it accordingly. Make your delivery extraordinary.

Finally, remember this little rhyme about money and honey, and be reassured. As you practice the principles in this book, you will have both: *money* and *honey*.

You Can't Buy Love

There was a lad from Donnegal.
He loved his Tess more than any gal.
A rich man is what she wanted.
So his cash is what he flaunted.
They wed and the years did fly.
They relished what money could buy.
With time far spent,
They once did lament...
"In our life, there's much money.
"In our love, there's no honey.
*   ...Alas, we are poor indeed.*

Leverage Key 23

Exuberance

Exuberance: *Extreme joyfulness and vigor*. Question: What to do with it and what to do about it?

I received one of those phone calls nearly all author/ consultants appreciate. "We need a keynote speaker to deliver a special message that will uplift our people and help us launch a new business development campaign." The call was from a B. Dalton Bookseller executive. He went on to explain that their sales had gone flat and they were looking for any and all new ways to stimulate a return to sales growth. If the keynote were successful, I would be asked to take the show on the road and address several regional groups within the company. Not only was this a keynote opportunity, but it was the opportunity make an honest-to-goodness, lasting impact on the success of this fine company with whom I had shopped for years.

When the Wind Stops Blowing, Start Rowing

The company had identified this theme for their employee conferences: *When the wind stops blowing, start rowing.* To help propel this theme forward, each employee was given a handsome gold-plated pin with the image of a person in a rowboat, holding oars in each hand. The message of the pin: Each employee is in the B. Dalton boat, the wind has stopped, the sails (sales) have gone limp, and the boat is going nowhere fast. In the real world, I know some employees would ask, "Well, when is management going to do something about the boat or the wind?" Or they would wonder, "Do we have a diesel engine as back up for the wind/ sail thing?" Of course the answer needed to be that no one is coming. We must each pick up the oars and help row OUR boat.

This is exactly what happened in Flagstaff, Arizona. One young man responded by proposing various ways to increase customer traffic to their local store, situated in a stand-alone strip mall. They needed to attract customers away from the big mall, which housed their principal competitor's store. Flagstaff is located in the vicinity of several Indian reservations and is the crossroads for many Native American artists. The exuberant young employee came up with the idea to display Native American artifacts throughout the store to make the store more appealing and to create a win/win relation-ship with the local artists who would be delighted to have their works showcased at a popular retail outlet. The idea worked. People were attracted to the new window displays and found that the inside of the store had taken on more of a mini-museum quality that was much less "commercial." Book sales began to increase. Employee enthusiasm increased. The young man who was the instigator decided to promote the store more aggressively. He designed an inexpensive, but attractive flier and proceeded to place these on the windshields of cars parked at the mall.

Within just minutes, it seemed, there was an angry manager from the mall bookstore on the phone talking to a newly perplexed B. Dalton Bookseller manager, while his now bewildered employee stood by and listened. The angry manager pointed out that the mall was private property and the fliers were placed on cars without authorization. The order was given to the B. Dalton employee to immediately remove all fliers, which he did.

The Moment of Truth at B. Dalton

It was a sad day at the B. Dalton store. The store was beautiful, sales were up, but morale was way down after this close encounter at the mall. Then, the store staff received word that their regional manager would soon be visiting the store for an inspection. The young man who had been the driving force behind the new store beautification campaign had mixed feelings. He believed the regional manager would like the store, but he just knew he would be hauled on the carpet for messing up the flier thing at the mall.

The day of the big visit came. Immediately upon entering the store, the B. Dalton regional manager asked for the young man responsible for the Native American décor. The employee came forward. As he

did, he heard the question, "Are you the one who
came up with idea?" "Yes sir." "Well, I think the
store looks great. About the flier thing at the mall..."
"I know, sir, I am so sorry. I didn't mean to mess that
up." "Oh, no, you don't understand..." (At this moment,
the morale of one young man and that of B. Dalton
employees across the country hung in the balance.
Depending on what the regional manager said next,
the fears of cynics would be confirmed or a belief-
building wave would be sent across the company.) The
manager continued, "You don't understand. Keep it
up. This is the spirit we need. *And don't worry; we
have bail money for creative employees.*" Word did
travel like a tidal wave. The "start rowing" message
was not just a slogan. Management actually believed
the goal they had spoken. They were walking the talk.

Do we encourage others to row the boat? Do we
forget they're even in the boat? Do they perceive that
we're primarily waiting to chastise them if they *rock
the boat*?

Exuberance: Zest for Life

Oh how precious is enthusiasm. How powerful is
its full-grown, live-life-out-loud cousin called exuberance? Would you rather have to periodically calm
down an associate or spend endless hours trying to
build a fire under someone with no vigor and little
zest for life?

When a child is especially happy and comes running
to its parents, they often ask, "Honey, what happened?
Why are you so happy?" We ask this as if happiness
is a surprise phenomenon. The child is likely to reply,

"I don't know. I'm just happy." Then comes a puzzled parent look and, "Oh, that's wonderful. Go play." I can imagine the conversation continuing after the child skips across the lawn. Father turns to mother and says, "Honey, are you happy?" "Oh, I don't know." "What can I do to help you be happy?" "Oh, nothing, I'm okay, really." And then they return to waiting for the bluebird of happiness to pay them a visit. A child doesn't need a reason to be happy.

The word *exuberance* was chosen because it is not a commonly used term. Perhaps it is an uncommon phenomenon. Why is this so? Is it possible that many of us grown-ups don't know what to think of boundless enthusiasm? Does it frighten us or embarrass us? If it does, we turn away from it or discourage it and therefore there is less of it. Perhaps the bluebird has come and we didn't recognize it.

Next time a child or a grown-up comes to you smiling and happy, don't ask why they are so happy. Tell them how much you appreciate their joyful outlook on life. Ask them to sit with you and let it rub off. Discovering joy is finding leverage. It lifts many burdens. It opens many hearts.

Leverage Key 24

━━━━━━━━━━━━━━━

What's Love Got to Do With It?

Is love leverage? Ever since I was a boy, I've been taught that love makes the world go around. Well, if it can make the world go around, it can certainly lift it up as well. I'm sure Archimedes would agree.

The Surprising Success Secret of a Very Powerful Man

I do not recall how I was so fortunate as to gain an audience with Trammell Crow. His great name is synonymous with real estate development. The company he founded is a foremost leader in the industry worldwide. I visited the Trammell Crow offices in Dallas, Texas, as part of research I was doing for an earlier book about "taking pride in your work." An elevator ride took me to the umpteenth floor. Upon entering the executive suite, I was greeted by a cheerful receptionist who asked me to wait briefly for Mr. Crow. I must admit that I expected a tall, imposing figure to emerge in a blue, pin-striped suit. Within a few minutes, a grandfatherly figure came walking across the waiting area toward me. He was of average height and a slender build. He appeared to be in his late 60s or early 70s and was wearing a rather ordinary brown suit.

Mr. Crow welcomed me and asked me to sit down. We chatted briefly. I was charmed by the man and yet slightly intimidated by his immense success and influence. As my confidence grew, I asked him my big question of the day: "Mr. Crow, you are a very successful and influential man. To what do you most attribute this success?" Without hesitation, he replied, "Young man, I have great people working for me. As you came up the elevator to my offices, you passed by the floors where several thousand of them work. The secret to my success is that these people all know that I love them." I was thrilled and humbled by his remark. I thanked him for the short but forever meaningful interview. By the way, I very recently found the following quotation from Trammell Crow on his Website: "There must always, always be a burning in your heart to achieve. In the quiet of your solitude, close your eyes, bow your head, grit your teeth, clench your fists, ache in your heart, vow and dedicate yourself to achieve, to achieve."

Mr. Crow's determination to achieve coupled with a love for those who shared his dream have doubly blessed the lives of many, I know. His success reflects a balance of leadership attributes.

Placing Service Before Self-Interest

What has love got to do with it? The answer: Everything. Love does make the world go around. Its extreme opposite, hatred, makes the world stop in its tracks. Where there is no love, selfishness, arrogance, greed, and the lust for power take over. The most intriguing challenge to great leadership is this: To place service over self-interest. Some embrace this notion as a noble ideal. Some perceive it as totally naïve. Others struggle with it as perhaps important, but too much at odds with human nature to be practical. Each of us as leaders must examine our motives and ask this simple question: What approach to life, to business, and to my associates will tap my greatest potential and do the most good? The alternative is to ask: What approach will help me maximize my fame and fortune? Without love, leadership may be a masquerade. With a love for humanity, for the beauty of the world, for the grand adventure of it all, a leader does rise above human nature to make a mark upon the world that will be for good.

What is love? The romanticized notions of love are delicious and desirable. Beyond this, love is a level of concern and admiration for others that transcends appreciation and friendship. This love puts a priority on relationships that engage the deepest of human emotions, those of caring, with a desire to lift up and to build.

Take Your Business Where You Feel Loved

I often tell my client groups that I love my customers. Many chuckle. Some get it. Some don't. I go on to explain that if you don't love your customers, you've probably never started your own business. I recall when Sharon and I founded Cornerstone, we prayed for a customer, any customer, just someone who would believe in us and to whom we could send an invoice so that we could feed our children. One of my great friends, Lynn Fairbanks, once told me that you can have all the talent in the world, but unless someone gives you the opportunity to use it, it is not of much value. Oh how I love those who have believed in me and given me an opportunity to use my talents.

One of my colleagues teaches this: You usually take your business where you feel infinitely more loved. You want to be treated graciously and lovingly by those who serve you. In addition to their competent attention to your needs, you want their TLC (tender loving care) when your car is broken, when you are trying to sell your old home to avoid double house payments, or when you are dining out with someone very important to you.

To draw upon Mr. Crow's earlier quotation, it is often love that stimulates the "burning in your heart" or the "ache in your heart." *Why* would your heart burn or ache? I propose that these powerful emotions are primarily about two things: realizing your potential and making a difference. Why realize your potential? Because you can't bear to see it wasted. Why make a difference? Because someone out there will be better off and appreciate what you have done. If you love those you serve, the difference you make will be profound. And if you realize your potential, you will love who you have become.

A Story of Love Lost

Consider what's wrong with this picture. I was teaching in San Bernardino, California. A farming supervisor approached me at the break to ask, "Mr. Checketts, I supervise many part-time, temporary workers. What I need to know is how do I get these people to be as motivated as our regular, full-time employees?" I then asked, "My friend, do you treat your part-time, temporary workers the same way you treat your regular, full-time employees?" He replied, "Of course not, they're just temporary workers." The moral of the story is: We teach others how to treat us.

The divine teacher of Nazareth taught, "By this shall all men know that ye are my disciples, if ye have love one to another." Whoever's disciple you may be or whoever may follow you, your bond of deepest respect and of love will distinguish who you are. Love will lift you up.

Leverage Key 25

Your Value Proposition

We talk a great deal about "value added" in business. Life is about value added. A personal value proposition is the answer to this question: *Why* would I want to join forces with you, do business with you, trust you, make a commitment to you, and share the dream with you?

Your Elevator Speech: Be Ready

I remember being challenged to always have a 30- to 90-second "elevator speech" to use if I ever got on the elevator and the President of United States were standing inside, looked straight at me and said, "I need a new Cabinet member. Tell me in 60 seconds why I should consider you."

Your value proposition begins with you—who you are, what you are prepared to do, and what you can achieve that makes a difference. Can you sum it all up?

Value Proposition: A Weighty Matter for Me

Until I was 16, I was not known for my physical prowess but rather for some reasonable intellectual ability. My parents and teachers appreciated this fact. Unfortunately, for purposes of my social life, the girls seemed to admire muscle-bound jocks more than me. And to further complicate things, the jocks made fun of me. It all started in third grade with one bully who would chase me around the schoolyard, finally catch me, and throw me to the ground. He would then sit on my chest and stuff grass in my shirt and mouth while the other kids watched. Luckily, I was not permanently scarred by this abuse. But I realized I needed to change my value proposition.

About age 16, a wonderful transformation began to occur. I owe it all (almost all) to the Weider company that manufactures barbells. I purchased a set and proceeded to follow the instructions for body building religiously, plus my mother fed me well. My appetite grew. My mother fed me even more. I grew to 6 feet 2 inches tall and 195 pounds by the beginning of my junior year in high school. What was even more important was that the 195 pounds was mostly muscle. Yeah, baby! My value proposition had grown from *smart* to *smart and strong*. My favorite new pastime was to invite some of the young studs from high school over to my back yard, throw 120 pounds onto the barbell and ask them press the barbell over their heads. They would laugh, grab the barbell with two hands, and then easily press it into the air. I would then grab the same barbell (not dumbbell) in the very center of the bar with *One* hand and press it into the air. Others tried to match my feat. They would grunt, wobble, stumble, and then drop the barbell without success. The jocks stopped teasing me.

Can You Lift You?

One of the great benchmarks (no pun intended) in weightlifting is to bench press your own body weight and more, which I was soon able to do. This was such a symbolic goal. It meant that *I could lift me*. Wow! Perhaps this is a bedrock opportunity represented by the Archimedes Factor—to have enough leverage to lift *you*. Until you can lift *you*, it is difficult to lift others. Your value proposition becomes your commitment to what it is you intend to lift about yourself and for others. Consider…

- ✓ Lift your sights.
- ✓ Lift your standards.
- ✓ Lift your spirit.

Then, with the help of others you serve….

- ✓ Lift the quality of your own team work experience.
- ✓ Lift the reputation of your company in the eyes of your customers.
- ✓ Lift the prospects for peace and prosperity all around.

How High Can You Lift You?

Inside this commitment to lift is a fundamental requirement that we have already addressed here and there, in a variety of ways. It is faith.

- ✓ To have faith in yourself.
- ✓ To have faith in your abilities and your potential.
- ✓ To have faith in your purpose and your vision.
- ✓ To have faith in those you love and who love you.
- ✓ To have faith in all of your associates and in other resources you may call upon.
- ✓ To have faith in God and the forces at work in the universe.

As you make this commitment to lifting and to the faith you need to do it, your value proposition will become clear. Others will trust you and willingly join forces with you to accomplish much more than you could do on your own.

Value Propositions of Heroic Proportions

Remember the great leaders we have discussed in this book: Henry V, Gandhi, Lawrence of Arabia, Thomas Edison, Paul Revere, George Washington, Moses, Ramses, Mother Teresa, Trammell Crow, Jeff Bezos,

J.K. Rowling, and others. Each of these has a value proposition written across their reputation.

- ✓ Henry V: to stand by his men.
- ✓ Gandhi: to peacefully lead his people to the freedom they deserved.
- ✓ Lawrence of Arabia: to stir passion and empower his followers.
- ✓ Thomas Edison: to light the way for the world.
- ✓ Paul Revere: to connect a colonial community to defend its destiny.
- ✓ George Washington: to meet the goal and fulfill the destiny.
- ✓ Moses: to let faith conquer all.
- ✓ Ramses: so let it be written, so let it be done...to lay the foundation for Egyptian tourism.
- ✓ Mother Teresa: to abandon no one.
- ✓ Trammel Crow: to achieve, to achieve, and to love those who help you do it.
- ✓ Jeff Bezos: to make it work whatever it takes...and get the books there a day early.
- ✓ J.K. Rowling: to entice millions of "kids" to discover the wonder of books.
- ✓ And remember the young sales clerk at B. Dalton Bookseller: to grab the oars and row.

We would follow these leaders. Their value proposition was and is still clear today. It is clear what their leverage has been. In some way, each of these leaders has lifted us up. Their faith in themselves, in others, and in their purpose has been a force in the world.

By the way, I still lift weights. Perhaps it is symbolic. It has to start somewhere. It starts with me.

Give me a lever long enough and a place to stand, and I could lift the world. Archimedes, you're my hero. Thanks for the great inspiration.

Conclusion

Today, as I drove back to my office from a client coaching session, I followed a brand new, midnight blue Dodge Durango SUV down the highway. Its appearance was sleek and muscular. The inward-curving side fenders on the front of the vehicle were unique. I realized how much hard work, creativity, and money goes into developing a new car model. I also realized how much Americans, and increasingly our fellow citizens of the world, love their automobiles.

My mind wandered from the Durango to the whole idea in our society that the wonders of technology will solve so many of our problems and make us happy. Then my reflections moved on to the problems we do face: the threat and the fear of terrorism, natural disasters, global economic challenges, drugs, disease, educational reform, and poverty. What an amazing age we live in.

The Age of Fear?

We face such great challenges and yet we have great leverage to help us solve these problems. The heroes of our society may be the engineers and the scientists who are unlocking the keys to faster, sleeker, longer lasting, more affordable everything. Some form of "technology" touches every aspect of our lives it seems. We hope it holds the answers. We have discovered how to reengineer parts of our bodies. We each carry an encyclopedia of information in our PDA's. Video games simulate everything. Pills change moods, stop pain, cure disease, and stimulate romance. Our worlds vibrate in our purses or pockets as the cell phone "rings," only it doesn't ring, it plays a symphony or a rapper's punch line.

So many of us seem to be searching for something. We watch Reality TV. We hope a popular talk show host will spell it out and reassure us, or a stand-up comic will provide some relief. We look for meaning and purpose. In the end, we usually manage to keep hope alive, juggle the many priorities of our lives, and move on. Still we search.

What Is the Answer to It All?

A little over a week ago, I sat in the office of a great friend and colleague. Playing in the background was the music of Jeffrey Gaines. I had not heard him before, but I will listen again. The lyrics of his soulful song were punctuated by the line, "There's got to be some hero in me." The words grabbed my attention, uplifted me, distracted me, and continued to haunt me. After all the gadgets have been purchased...after all the pills have been popped...after all the Reality TV...after Batman has saved the world...

There's got to be some hero in me.

Do I still hold the key to me? Are the answers out there somewhere, or in me? Will a UPS truck deliver my happiness, or will I? Can Homeland Security save our nation, or will we? Where's the answer to the problems we see? *There's got to be some hero in me.*

I wrote this book to help you be the hero you need. A man once asked God why he hadn't done something about all the pain and suffering in the world. God replied, "I have. I sent you." This is not a clever, inspirational play on words. It is true. God is operating in His universe through you. All you need is leverage to lift your world. As you do, you will help others discover their leverage as well. You are the key to the happiness you seek. The wonders of technology are levers you use, not the answers. You are the most wondrous creation in the universe. You are the answer. This is not the Age of Fear. Archimedes spoke the truth. He would agree, *with a lever long enough and a place to stand, you will lift the world*. There is a hero. It's you.

The Genesis of a Book

Oracle Corporation is a powerhouse company with immense global influence. I thank Oracle for a key connection that served as the catalyst for creating this book. Other important factors also contributed to the genesis of the book.

It was George Anderson, my dedicated high school math teacher, who first taught me "the Archimedes Factor." The word "leverage" became an important element of my vocabulary. While writing the book, I was also reading Malcolm Gladwell's breakthrough book, *The Tipping Point*, which perfectly illustrates the results of applying leverage to create tipping points. Steve Chandler has been the chief cheerleader for the book. However, the folks at Oracle provided the final spark that lit the *Leverage* fire.

The phone rang. It was my son, Vance, on the phone. He is a member of the Oracle team. He informed me that his team leaders at Oracle, Jeff Abbott and John Fichtner, were planning a meeting in Scottsdale, Arizona, (not far from my home) and wanted to include a motivational keynote presentation in their agenda. I contacted Jeff and John. We struck the right chord. They challenged me with this: "Darby, you realize that there will be a very high-powered group of people in that room. These are the experts who support key sales and client relationships for Oracle around the globe." I accepted their challenge and hung up the phone. I leaned back in my chair and made a colorful exclamation. Then, I silently apologized for my impulse and gave thanks for this cool opportunity.

I certainly knew the visibility of Oracle as a global company and the high-energy nature of the Oracle organization, starting with their amazing CEO and his leadership team. I next said to myself, "Darby, you can't blow this keynote, that's for sure." I realized my eldest son would be sitting in the audience. What would his buddies turn to him and say when I was finished? I knew this had to be a *knock-their-socks-off* keynote. So, I went to work on my presentation. The title of the keynote was "How to Instill the Vision, Build Partnerships, and Do the Impossible." I have always taught my clients that nothing is impossible with the right partnerships. Partnerships are *super leverage* in facing the toughest challenges in business and in life. As the word *leverage* popped into my mind, I visualized the handout for the keynote with the image of a person holding a lever and lifting the world. For my Oracle audience, "the world" would be the world of their customers.

The rest is history. The keynote went very well. I connected with these hard-working professionals from Oracle in a way that made me feel a part of their family.

I thank them for their zeal and for their enthusiastic response to my message. Plus, Vance's key associates turned to him and said the words I had designed into my vision of "the ideal scenario." I was doubly pleased that I had made my son proud. His great company is big on *commitment* and we all know what powerful leverage true commitment is. Thank you, Oracle.

Index

A

achievement, goal, 30
Acropolis, 23
affirmations, 38
Africa, 30-32, 70
    West, 32
Agreement, 147-150
alignment, cultural, 36
Amazon.com, 155, 168-169
Archimedes, 19-22, 34, 38,
    63, 80, 126, 141,
    160-165, 195, 205
Arizona, 41, 46, 86, 134
    Flagstaff, 190
    Phoenix, 50, 64
    Scottsdale, 51
army, the British, 102
astronauts, 21

Athens, 19
autobahn, 153, 181

B

B. Dalton Booksellers,
    189-192, 205
behaviors, 36
benefits, organizational, 37
Bezos, Jeff, 155, 168-169,
    204-205
bombshell, emotional, 47
bookends, 35, 37-38, 43
    organizational, 36
Branagh, Kenneth, 81
British, 140
Bryner, Yul, 141
Built to Last, 167

C

California, San Bernardino, 199
cancer, 47-49, 51, 176
Capital Development Board
 of Illinois, 153
Carrey, Jim, 183, 185-186
Carrier, William Haviland, 169
cashews, Kirkland, 64-67
CEOs, 35, 159
Chandler, Steve, 60, 100,
 111, 116
Charles, Ray, 57-61
Chi-chen-itza,
 Sacred Well of, 33
Circle of Innovation, The, 95
City Slickers, 45
clots, blood, 47
Collins, Jim, 16, 167
Colorado Rockies, 86
Colorado, 50
commitment, 139-145, 148,
150
conscious thankfulness,
 euphoric states of, 49
consciousness, elevation of,
49
Constitution, the United
 States, 168, 172
Costco, 64-67
costumes, Thai, 90
Crystal, Billy, 45, 51
Culture, Corporate, 35, 36
*Customer Astonishment
 Handbook,* 100

Customer Astonishment, 16,
 75, 153
Customer Champion, 75, 76

D

Dancing in Peanut Butter, 100
*Deep Survival: Who Lives,
 Who Dies,* 144
Delaware, 73, 140-142
discipline, 80
 principles of, 79
DNA, corporate, 35
Dodge, 207
Donnegal, 188
dreams, 30, 183
DuPont, 103

E

Ecuador, 46
Edison, Thomas, 73, 204-205
education, Ivy League, 28
Egypt, Pharaoh of,
 see Ramases
endorphins, 49
explorers, 22
Exuberance, 189-193

F

Factor, the Archimedes,
 19-23, 25, 203
fashion, Greek, 20
Fischer, David Hackett, 101
Fisher, Roger, 101

Five Arenas of Live, 45-55
Focus, Customer, 36
food,
  Greek, 19
  Thai, 90
Force Fields, 131-137
Force(s),
  Active, 133
  Driving, 132
  Receptive, 132-134, 136
  Reconciling, 133, 136
  Restraining, 132
Force, The, 97
fulcrum, 21
functions, bodily, 49

G

Gaines, Jeffrey, 208
Gandhi, 122-123, 204-205
Gandhi, 81
Gates, Bill 159
Gergen, David, 159
Getting to Yes, 101
goals,
  daring, 71
  high-priority, 51
God, 49, 53, 55, 87
Golden Rule, The, 128, 130
Gonzales, Laurence, 144
Good to Great, 16
Greeks, 22-23
guides, relationship
  investment, 100

H

habit(s), life-long, 32
Henry V, 122-124, 204-205
Henry V, 81
heroes, 120-123
heroin, 58
Heston, Charlton, 141
Hicks, Ben, 86
honesty, 80
  principles of, 79
Hong Kong, 66
Hoover Dam, 176
humility, 121-123, 143

I

Ikeja, 39
industry, Egyptian tourist, 141
influence, 119-126
iPod, 70

J

Jefferson, Thomas, 168
Jesus Christ, 43, 50
Jiffy Lube, 54
John Muir trail, 33
Jordan, Michael, 92

K

Kilimanjaro, 27
King, Larry, 70
King, Larry, 72
Kingsley, Ben, 81

L

Lagos, 39
Lawrence of Arabia,
          122-123, 204-205
Lawrence of Arabia, 81
Lawrence, T.E., 81
leadership. 119-126
learning, 159-165
levers, 21
lists, to-do, 54
London, 27, 31, 147
lymphoma, 47

M

Mars, 156-158
mathematicians, 21, 22
mathematics, 20
mechanisms, 167-172, 173
Mexico City, 93
Militiamen, Pennsylvania, 140
Moses, 141, 204-205
Mother Teresa, 77, 93, 204-205
Mount Everest. 31
Mount Kilimanjaro, 31-33
MRIs, 47
Murray, W.H., 71
music, 49

N

NASCAR, 89
National Geographic, 29, 65
Navajo, 64

Nazareth, 199
Needs, Maslow's Hierarchy
          of, 77
New York City, 140
Nicaragua, 33
Nigeria, 27, 31, 33-34, 39, 40,
          42-43
nodes, lymph, 47
Northern Arizona
          University, 87

O

O'Toole, Peter, 81
officers, British, 102
oncologists, 49, 51
Ownership Spirit, 60
ownership, 111-117, 140

P

Palance, Jack, 45, 46
Parthenon, 19
partnerships, 97-98, 173-179
people-centered, 75-80
Perspective, 105
Peters, Tom, 95
pharaohs, 142
philosophers, 77
          Greek, 20
philosophies, 132
physicists, 21, 22
plan(s), financial, 36
poetry, 32
points, tipping, 25

Porras, Jerry, 167
PowerPoint, 53, 134
priorities, 46, 52, 55
programs, Web-based

purpose, 80
    Core, 36-37, 144
    high, 71
pyramid, 141-142

R

rafting, river, 50
Ramses, 141-142, 204-205
Ray, 57-61
Red Mountain Freeway, 174
Red Sea, 33, 141-142
*Relationshift, 50 Ways to
    Create,* 102
Retton, Mary Lou, 87
Revere, Paul, 101-102,
    204-205
Rio Coco, 33
Rio Salado College, 174
Rowling, J.K., 155, 204-205
Royal Aeronautical Society, 147

S

scans, CT, 47
Seal, Navy, 151-152
Singapore, 96
situations,
    future, 154
    parent, 154

six degrees of separation, 63
SLIBW-SLIBD, 141
So Let It Be Written,
    see SLIBW-SLIBD
soldiers,
    Iraqi, 51
    Afghan, 51
    American, 51
South Carolina, 48
sphere, geometric, 23
St. Louis Cardinals, 86
stewardship, 111-117, 140
systems,
    owner, 112-114
    victim, 112-114

T

technology, computer, 108
Ten Commandments, The, 141
Thailand, 90
Thinking, 151-158
thread, Kevlar, 71
Tibet, 181
Tillman, Pat, 86
Tipping Point, The, 16, 101
tolerance, zero, 79
tool(s)
    goal setting, 30
    dreaming, 30
    make-it-happen, 30
Trump, Donald, 87
truth, 127-130

U

U.S. News & World Report, 159
United Kingdom, 27
United Nations World Food
        Program, 33
United States, 32, 43
UPS, 209
Ury, William, 101
Utah, 46

V

vocabulary of patterns, 152
Victoria Island, 40

W

Wall Street Journal, The, 29
Washington, George, 73,
        139-141, 168, 204-205
wealth, 181-188
What is Theoretically
        Possible?
        see also, WITP
Why-to, 37
Williamson, Marianne, 69
WITP, 103-109

Z

zones, Earth's climatic, 31

About the Author

Darby Checketts grew up on a small ranch in South Phoenix, Arizona, where his family raised quarter horses, sheep, turkeys, watermelons, and dates. He and Sharon are the parents of seven fantastic children: Natalie, Vance, Denise, Cheryl, Ken, Brent, and Matt. Darby and Sharon live in Mesa, Arizona, where they manage the activities of Cornerstone Professional Development, which they founded in 1985. Together with their various partners, they expound the principles of *Customer Astonishment* and *Leverage*. Darby is president of the company and also serves as its principal trainer and strategist. He has worked with hundreds of organizations, large and small, around the globe. Literally millions of individuals have benefited, directly and indirectly, from his in-person teachings, his books, and various other publications. His professional career began with Ford Motor Company and includes experience with several other companies where he served in a variety of management and professional positions. He has traveled throughout 47 of the 50 United States and 25 countries on five continents. Darby's first loves are God, family, and country, followed by his love of helping his clients achieve their goals and by opportunities for community service and travel. *Leverage* is Darby's sixth book. His other recent books are:

Customer Astonishment: 10 Secrets to World-Class Customer Care.

Dancing in Peanut Butter: A Guide for Handling "the Stuff that Happens" in Life.

Please visit *www.LeverageKeys.com*. Telephone Darby at (480) 654-0811. He is available to support you as a coach, strategist, speaker, and all-around source of education and inspiration. He is also a *connector* to those who have other wisdom you may wish to access.